Shelby Foote

THE CIVIL WAR

A NARRATIVE

Shelby Foote

THE CIVIL WAR

A NARRATIVE

9

★ ★ ★

MINE RUN
TO MERIDIAN

40th Anniversary Edition

BY SHELBY FOOTE
AND THE EDITORS OF TIME-LIFE BOOKS,
ALEXANDRIA, VIRGINIA

*All these were honoured in their generations,
and were the glory of their times.*

*There be of them,
that have left a name behind them,
that their praises might be reported.*

*And some there be, which have no memorial;
who are perished, as though they had never been;
and are become as though they had never been born;
and their children after them.*

*But these were merciful men,
whose righteousness hath not been forgotten.*

*With their seed shall continually remain
a good inheritance,
and their children are within the covenant.*

*Their seed standeth fast,
and their children for their sakes.*

*Their seed shall remain for ever,
and their glory shall not be blotted out.*

*Their bodies are buried in peace;
but their name liveth for evermore.*

— ECCLESIASTICUS XLIV

Contents

★ ★ ★

★

Prologue

———— ❦ ————

★ ★ ★ **A**s 1864 opened, both Lincoln and Davis had much on their minds. The bloody conflict between their two nations had been a seesaw affair during the previous six months. Central and western Tennessee were secured for the Union when, after forceful urgings from Washington, William Rosecrans executed a brilliant series of maneuvers to force Braxton Bragg south from Tullahoma, then beyond Chattanooga. Thinking that Bragg was on the run, Rosecrans chased too fast and too far, and Bragg, reinforced by two divisions from Virginia under Longstreet, handed the Federals a bloody two-day defeat along Chickamauga Creek, driving them back into Chattanooga. Bragg failed to follow up the victory, but he did invest the city, making it nearly impossible for the starving Yankees holed up there to get the supplies from the nearby depot at Stevenson, Alabama. Meanwhile, John Hunt Morgan's raid to threaten as far north as Cincinnati had been repulsed and most of his cavalrymen captured; Ambrose Burnside's Army of the Cumberland had occupied Knoxville; and Nathaniel Banks' attempt to expand Federal control in Texas came to a standstill at Sabine Pass.

In the east, Robert E. Lee took the offensive against George Meade near Culpeper, Virginia, beginning a one-month period of indecisive maneuverings in which Lee forced Meade to retreat, but could not destroy him before he reached strong positions behind Bull Run. Confederates took heavy losses at Bristoe Station, while northern cavalry was routed near Buckland Mills. All the while, Yankees were closing the ring ever tighter around Charleston, South Carolina — they had taken Folly Island, and U.S. ironclads continued their bombardment of Fort Sumter. But Federal forces, led by black troops of the 54th Massachusetts, met a crushing defeat in an attempt to take Battery Wagner on Morris Island, although subsequent shellings soon forced the rebels to abandon the position.

Disgusted by Rosecrans' failure at Chickamauga, Lincoln ordered Grant to take command at Chattanooga and he went to work immediately, opening the Cracker Line — his supply route to the Stevenson depot. With food and equipment pouring in, Grant began to restore the morale and fighting trim of his troops. Physical conditions for the Confederate besiegers had been almost as bad as those for the Yankee besieged. But the situation was made even worse by the bickering among rebel commanders. In spite of having won what some called the South's greatest victory of the war, there were calls for Bragg's ouster following his failure to pursue the fleeing enemy into and beyond Chattanooga.

Bragg, sustained by President Davis, fired several of his complaining subordinates and sent off his best, James Longstreet, to retake Knoxville.

In early November, Meade moved south, only to be stopped by Lee's forces at Mine Run — and both then settled into winter camps. Later that month, Grant was ready and so was his army. First driving the Confederates from Lookout Mountain and, the next day, storming rebel positions on Missionary Ridge, the Federals broke the siege and chased the rebels to the southeast until exhaustion and stiff resistance at Ringgold Gap ended the pursuit. Four days later, Longstreet's nearly month-long campaign to regain Knoxville failed as his troops struggled in the tripwires, trenches, and withering fire of the Federal defenses at Fort Sanders on the edge of the city.

In the new year, an ill-fated Federal attempt to invade central Florida was stymied at Olustee, and a full-scale cavalry raid to burn Richmond, and perhaps kill the Confederate president, ended in disaster and brought on a firestorm of controversy. Sherman's expedition into central Mississippi to wreak havoc on southern rail and road lines got as far as Meridian, where he was to have been joined by forces under William Sooy Smith. But Smith ran afoul of Forrest's rebel cavalry far shy of the rendezvous. After putting Meridian to the torch, Sherman withdrew into central Mississippi and eventually Vicksburg. In an attempt to break the Federal blockade at Charleston, the South experimented with the *H. L. Hunley* — the first submarine to sink an enemy vessel in battle — but the *Hunley,* too, went to the bottom.

Aware that he was up for reëlection in the fall and needed to consolidate his position, Lincoln deftly faced political opponents in his administration and convinced Congress that Ulysses S. Grant should come east to assume command of all the nation's armies. Davis did not match the action, but against his better judgment and to the surprise of everyone, Joseph Johnston was sent west and Bragg was called to Richmond as chief military adviser. While Lincoln called for an additional 500,000 troops, Davis could only increase the numbers in his ranks by lowering and raising the draft ages to seventeen and fifty. Political opposition and widespread despair led Davis to take political and legal steps that seriously jeopardized the morale he sought to improve and the very existence of the nation he intended to unify.

★   ★   ★

Shelby Foote

*B*y December 1863, nearly
50,000 men of African descent, like
these members of Company E, 4th
U.S. Colored Troops, had swelled
the ranks of the northern armies.

ONE

Mine Run;
Meade Withdraws

1863 ★ ★ ★ ★ ★ ★ **N**ews of the great Chattanooga victory, which had begun on Monday and ended on Wednesday, spread throughout the North on the following day, November 26. By coincidence, in a proclamation issued eight weeks earlier at the suggestion of a lady editor, Lincoln had called upon his fellow citizens "to set apart and observe the last Thursday of November next, as a day of thanksgiving and praise to our beneficent Father who dwelleth in the Heavens." Instituted thus "in the midst of a civil war of unequaled magnitude and severity," this first national Thanksgiving was intended not only as a reminder for people to be grateful for "the blessings of fruitful fields and healthful skies," but also as an occasion for them to "implore the interposition of the Almighty Hand to heal the wounds of the nation and to restore it, as soon as may be consistent with the Divine purposes, to the full enjoyment of peace, harmony, tranquillity, and Union." Now that word of what had happened yesterday on Missionary Ridge was added to the "singular deliverances and blessings" for which the public was urged to show its gratitude today, it seemed to many that the Almighty Hand had interposed already, answering a good part of their prayers in advance, and that the end so fervently hoped for might be considerably nearer than had been supposed when the proclamation was issued in early October, not quite two weeks after the shock of Chickamauga caused those hopes

★

to take a sudden drop. "This is truly a day of thanksgiving," Halleck wired Grant as the news of his latest triumph went out across the land and set the church bells ringing as wildly as they had rung after Donelson and Vicksburg.

Moreover, just as Thomas had taken his revenge for Chickamauga, so had Banks obtained by now at least a degree of recompense for the drubbing he had suffered in September, when he opened his campaign against coastal Texas with Franklin's botched attack on Sabine Pass. Revising his plan by reversing it, end for end, he decided to start with a landing near the Mexican border, then work his island-hopping way back east. It was true the pickings would be much slimmer at the outset, for there was little that far down the coast that was worth taking; but the objectives were unlikely to be as stoutly defended, and he would be moving toward, rather than away from, his New Orleans base of supplies, which should serve to encourage his men to fight harder and move faster, if for no other reason than to hasten their return. Accordingly, after sending Franklin's unhappy soldiers to Berwick for a renewed ascent of the Teche — an ascent that would end abruptly on November 3 at Grand Coteau, ten miles short of Opelousas, where the column was assaulted and driven back through Vermilionville to New Iberia by Richard Taylor and Tom Green, who lost 180 and inflicted 716 casualties, including the 536 fugitives they captured — he loaded aboard transports a 3500-man division, commanded by a Maine-born major general with the resounding name of Napoleon Jackson Tecumseh Dana,

who set out from New Orleans on October 26, escorted by three gunboats.

This time Banks went along himself, presumably to guard against snarls and hitches. At any rate there were none. On November 2 — the day before Franklin was thrown into sudden reverse at Grand Coteau — Dana put his troops ashore at Brazos Santiago, off the mouth of the Rio Grande, and though he encountered practically no resistance, the graybacks having been withdrawn to thicken the defenses in East Texas, Banks did not let this tone down the announcement of his achievement. "The flag of the Union floated over Texas today at meridian precisely," he notified Washington. "Our enterprise has been a complete success." Four days later he occupied Brownsville, just under thirty miles inland, opposite Matamoros, and sent for the puppet governor Andrew Hamilton, who had been waiting off-stage all this time and who was established there at the southernmost tip of the state and the nation, along with his gubernatorial staff of would-be cotton factors, before the month was out. Meanwhile Banks had followed up his initial success with a series of landings on Mustang and Matagorda islands, thus gaining control of Aransas Pass and Matagorda Bay. But that was all; that was as far as he got on his way back east. Galveston and the mouth of the Brazos River were too strongly held for him to attack them with Dana's present command, reduced as it was by garrison detachments, and Halleck could not be persuaded to accede to requests for reinforcements. All Banks had gained for his pains these past three months,

Captured and occupied by Banks' Federals in November 1863, Brownsville, Texas, at the mouth of the Rio Grande, was reopened for commerce the following February.

including the drubbing at Sabine Pass, was a couple of dusty border towns and a few bedraggled miles of Texas beach, mostly barren dunes, which he described as "inclement and uncomfortable, in consequence of the sterility of the soil and the violence of the northers."

Despite the flamboyance with which they were announced — "My most sanguine expectations are more than realized," Banks had proclaimed after occupying Brownsville; "Everything is now as favorable as could be desired" — the authorities in Washington were not inclined to include these shallow coastal lodgments, amounting in fact to little more than pinpricks along one leathery flank of the Texas elephant, among those things for which the nation should be thankful on its first Thanksgiving. Hamilton governed far too small and remote an area for his claims to be taken seriously, inside or outside the state, and it seemed to Lincoln, although he later thanked Banks politically for his "successful and valuable operations," that all the general had really done was shift some 3500 of his soldiers off to the margin of the map, where they were of about as much tactical value as if their transports had gone to the bottom of the Gulf with them aboard.

Halleck expressed an even dimmer view of the proceedings. "In regard to your Sabine and Rio Grande expeditions," he protested to the Massachusetts general, "no notice of your intention to make them was received here till they were actually undertaken." Old Brains was especially irked by the setback at Grand Coteau, which he saw as the result of an unwise division of force, occasioned by the unauthorized excursion down the coast. In his opinion, the Teche, the Atchafalaya, and the Red afforded the best approach to the Lone Star State, and though he understood that these streams were at present unusable even as supply routes, being practically dry at this season of the year, he wanted the entire command standing by for the early spring rise that would convert them into arteries of invasion. For this reason, as well as for the more general one that none were available, he flatly refused to send reinforcements for an attack on Galveston by the amphibious force which by now had worked its way back east to Matagorda, explaining testily that even if such an attack were successful — and even if the place did not turn out to be a trap, as it had done before — it still would be no more than a diversion from the true path of conquest.

Besides, there were nearer and larger frets, invoking more immediate concern; Knoxville, for example. "Remember Burnside," Lincoln had wired yesterday in response to Grant's announcement that victory was within reach at Chattanooga. He could breathe easier now, for while Longstreet's siege was apparently still in progress he knew that Grant, relieved of the presence of Bragg, was free to turn his attention to East Tennessee. But there was a still nearer fret, not sixty miles southwest of Washington, and though in this case the Union force was on the offensive, the Commander in Chief had learned from long experience that the strain of waiting for news of an expected success was quite as

Nathaniel P. Banks was a politically appointed general who served ten terms as a congressman from Massachusetts after the war.

great as waiting for news of an expected failure — particularly since experience had also taught him, all too often, that anticipated triumphs had a way of turning into the worst of all defeats; Chancellorsville, for instance. Meade at last had resumed his movement southward, having taken a two-week rest from the exertion of crossing the Rappahannock, and on this Thanksgiving morning the leading elements of his army were over the Rapidan, entering the gloomy western fringe of the Wilderness in whose depths Joe Hooker had come to grief in early May, just short of seven months ago.

His decision to cross and come to grips with Lee on that forbidding ground was based in part on a growing confidence proceeding from the fact that he had whipped him rather soundly in both of their recent face-to-face encounters, first at Bristoe Station and then at Rappahannock Bridge and Kelly's Ford. Moreover, there had come to hand on November 21 a detailed intelligence report which put the enemy strength at less than 40,000 effectives, as compared to his own 84,274 on that date. Actually, Lee's total was 48,586; Meade had just under, not just over, twice as many troops as his opponent. But in any case the preponderance was encouraging, and after four days of studying the figures and the map, he distributed on November 25 a circular directing his five corps commanders to be ready to march at 6 o'clock next morning, half an hour before sunrise.

Lee's two corps were strung out along the south bank of the river, one east and the other west of Clark's Mountain, their outer flanks respectively at Mine Run and Liberty Mills, some thirty miles apart; Meade's plan called for a crossing by the downstream fords, well beyond the Confederate right, and a fast march west, along the Orange Turnpike, for a blow at the rebel east flank before Lee could bring up his other corps in support. Unlike Hooker, Meade designed no feints or diversions, preferring to concentrate everything he had for the main effort. He relied entirely on speed, which would enable him to strike before his adversary had time to get set for the punch, and on the known numerical advantage, which would be far greater than two to one if he could mass and commit his fifteen infantry divisions before the rebel six achieved a concentration. All this was explained to the responsible subordinates, whose marches began on schedule from their prescribed assembly areas near Ely's and Germanna fords, well downstream from the apparently unsuspecting graybacks in their works across the way. Aside from a heavy morning fog, which screened the movement from enemy lookouts on Clark's Mountain — more evidence, it would seem, of the interposition of the Almighty Hand in favor of the Union on this Thanksgiving Day — the weather was pleasant, a bit chilly but all the more bracing for that, and the blue troops stepped out smartly along the roads and trails leading down to the various fords that had been assigned them so that a nearly simultaneous crossing could be made by the several columns. That too had been part of the design combining speed and power.

As always, there were hitches: only this time, with speed of such vital importance, they were even more exasperating than usual. What was worse, they began to crop up almost at the outset. Meade had planned with elaborate care, issuing eight-day rations to the men, for instance, to avoid the need for a slow-rolling wagon train that would take up a lot of road space and require a heavy guard; but he had neglected the human factor. In the present case, as it turned out, that factor was embodied in the person of William French, successor to Sickles as chief of the III Corps, which had been enlarged to three divisions, the same as the other four. A Maryland-born West Pointer nearing fifty, French was a tall, high-stomached man with an apoplectic look and a starchy manner, a combination that led an unadmiring staffer to remark that he resembled "one of those plethoric French colonels who are so stout, and who look so red in the face, that one would suppose someone had tied a cord tightly around their necks." So far in the war, though he had taken part in all the army's major fights except the two Bull Runs and Gettysburg, he had not distinguished himself in action. Today — and tomorrow too, for that matter, as developments would show — his performance was a good deal worse than undistinguished. Assigned to cross at Jacob's Ford, which meant that he would have the lead when the five corps turned west beyond the river, since it was the nearest of the three fords being used, he was not only late in arriving and slow in crossing, but when he found the opposite bank too steep for his battery horses to manage, he sent his artillery down to Germanna Ford and snarled the already heavy traffic there. It was dusk before he completed his crossing and called a halt close to the river, obliging those behind him to do likewise.

Next morning he stepped off smartly to make up for the time lost, then promptly took the wrong fork in the road and had to countermarch. By the time he got back on the right track, the sun was past the overhead and the movement was a full day behind schedule. Red-faced and angry, for Meade was prodding him hard by now, French set out once more through the woods that screened his approach to the rebel flank, supposedly a mile away, only to run into butternut skirmishers who obliged him to call a halt and deploy his lead division. Having done so, he started forward again; but not for long. Well short of the point he had been due to reach before he encountered anything more than an outpost handful of gray pickets, the firing stepped up and he found himself involved in a full-scale engagement with what seemed to be most of the rebels in the world. Apparently Lee had made good use of the time afforded him yesterday and today by the hitches that had slowed and stalled the greatly superior mass of bluecoats closing upon him through the woods on his downstream flank.

General William French, whose facial twitch won him the sobriquet "Old Blinky," bore much of the blame for the Union failure at Mine Run.

The southern commander had indeed made use of the time so generously allowed him. Informed by a scout on Thanksgiving Eve of the issue of eight-day rations across the way, he alerted his outposts to watch for a movement, upstream or down, and sat back to await developments. If the length of the numerical odds disturbed him, he could recall the victory he had scored against even longer odds, seven months ago, on practically this same ground. "With God's help," a young officer on his staff wrote home that night, "there shall be a Second Chancellorsville as there was a Second Manassas."

Next morning, when Stuart reported the Federals crossing in force by the lower fords, Lee sent word for Hill to take up the march from beyond Clark's Mountain to join Ewell, whose corps was on the right, and shifted army headquarters the following day from Orange to Verdiersville, a dozen miles east on the plank road. He did not know yet whether Richmond or the Army of Northern Virginia was Meade's objective, but in any case he decided that his best course was to move toward him, either for an interception or for a head-on confrontation. In the absence of Ewell, who was sick, the Second Corps was under Early; Lee told him to move eastward, down the pike toward Locust Grove, and keep going until he encountered something solid. That was how it came about that French, once he recovered his sense of direction and got back on the track that afternoon, found the woods a-boil with graybacks and was obliged to engage in an unscheduled and unwanted fight, one mile short of his immediate objective. Dusk ended the brief but savage action, in which each side lost better than 500 men, and Lee had Early fall back through the darkness to a previously selected position on the far side of Mine Run, which flowed due north into the Rapidan. Hill would arrive tomorrow and extend the line southward, taking post astride the turnpike and the plank road east of Verdiersville, while Early covered the approaches to Bartlett's Mill on the far left, near the river. Anticipating with satisfaction his first purely defensive full-scale battle since Fredericksburg, just two weeks short of a full year ago, Lee instructed his men to get busy with their shovels, preparing for a repetition of that butchery.

Coming up next day through a driving rain, which made for heavy marching, the bluecoats found themselves confronted by a seven-mile line of intrenchments whose approaches had been cleared for overlapping fields of fire. They took one look at the rebel works, sited forbiddingly along a ridge on the dominant west bank of the boggy stream, and decided that for the high command to send down orders for an assault would amount to issuing death warrants for most of the troops involved. Their generals rather thought so, too, when they came forward to reconnoiter, Warren and Sedgwick on the left and right, French in the center, and Sykes and Newton in reserve. By sundown the rain had slacked and stopped, giving way to a night so cold that the water froze in the men's canteens.

★

All next day the reconnaissance continued, and so did the spadework across the run. Meade was determined to try for a breakthrough, if one of his corps commanders would only find him a weak spot in the gray defenses. That night, when Sedgwick and Warren reported that they had found what he wanted on both flanks of the position, he issued instructions for an attack next morning. Sedgwick would open with his artillery at 7 o'clock on the right, attracting the enemy's attention in that direction, and Warren would launch an assault one hour later at the far end of the line, supported by French, who would feint at the rebel center, and by Newton, who would mass in his rear to help exploit the breakthrough. Similarly, Sykes would move up in close support of Sedgwick, whose bombardment was to be followed by an assault designed to shatter the Confederate left. With both flanks crumpled and no reserves on hand to shore them up, Lee would fall back in disarray and the blue reserves would hurry forward to complete his discomfort and destruction.

Waiting for the guns to stop their fuming,
some of the soldiers passed the time by writing their
names and addresses on bits of paper or chips of wood,
which they fastened inside their clothes . . .

So ordered, so attempted; Uncle John opened on schedule with all his guns, while down the line the troops assigned to the assault grew tenser by the minute as the time drew near for them to go forward. Whatever the generals back at headquarters might be thinking, the men themselves, crouched in the brush and peering out across the slashings at the icy creek which they would have to cross to get within reach of the butternut infantry — dug in along the ridge to await their coming and probably smiling with anticipation as they fondled their rifles or stood by their double-shotted cannon — did not like any part of the prospect now before them. For one thing, a man even lightly hit, out there in the clearing where no stretcher bearers could get to him, would probably die in this penetrating cold. For another, they judged that their deaths would be purposeless, for they did not believe that the assault could possibly succeed. Waiting for the guns to stop their fuming, some of the soldiers passed the time by writing their names and addresses on bits of paper or chips of wood, which they fastened inside their clothes; "Killed in action, Nov. 30, 1863," a few of the gloomier or more cynical ones among them added. However, just as the artillery left off roaring and they were about to step forward into chaos, a mes-

★

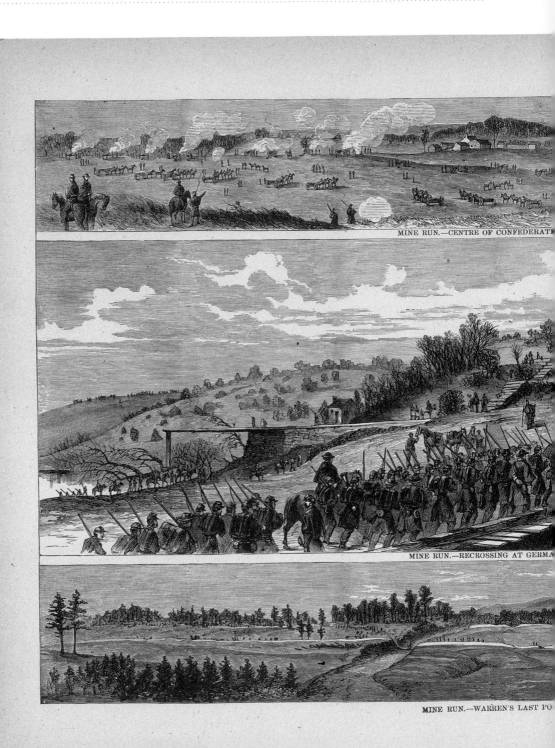

MINE RUN.—CENTRE OF CONFEDERATE

MINE RUN.—RECROSSING AT GERMA

MINE RUN.—WARREN'S LAST PO

522

HARPER'S PICTORIAL HISTORY OF THE CIVIL WAR.

[NOVEMBER, 1863.

Harper's Weekly ran these scenes to portray the Mine Run campaign: (top to bottom) Confederate artillery blazes away at unseen Yanks; Federals retreat across the Rapidan; and a view of Warren's position along Mine Run.

sage arrived from army headquarters: "Suspend the attack until further orders."

Later they found out why. On the far left, after discovering by day-light that the rebel defenses had been greatly strengthened overnight, Warren sent word that the assault he had deemed feasible yesterday would be suicidal today. Meade rode down to see for himself, found that he agreed with this re-vised assessment, and canceled the attack, both left and right. Grinning, the re-prieved troops discarded their improvised dogtags and thought higher than ever of Warren, who they were convinced had done the army as solid a service, in avoiding a disaster here today, as he had performed five months ago at Little Round Top or last month at Bristoc Station. What he had done, they realized, took a special kind of courage, and they were grateful not only to him but also to the commander who sustained him. Moreover, since supplies were getting low and a thaw would soften the crust of frozen mud without which no move-ment would be possible on the bottomless roads, Meade decided next day to withdraw the army over the same routes by which it had crossed the Rapidan, five days back, and entered this luckless woodland in the first place. So ordered, so done; the rearward movement began shortly after sunset, December 1, and continued through the night.

Glad as the departing bluecoats were to escape the wintry hug of the Wilderness, they were more fortunate than they knew. On November 30, the ex-pected assault not having been launched against his intrenchments, Lee had been summoned to the far right by Wade Hampton, who, recovered from his Gettysburg wounds and returned to duty, had discovered an opening for a blow at the Union left, not unlike the one Hooker had received in May on his oppo-site flank, a few miles to the east. Looking the situation over, the southern com-mander liked what he saw, but decided to wait before taking advantage of it. He felt sure that Meade would attack, sooner or later, and he did not want to pass up the near certainty of another Fredericksburg, even if it meant postponing a chance for another Chancellorsville. By noon of the following day, however, with the Federals still immobile in his front, he changed his mind. "They must be attacked; they must be attacked," he muttered. Accordingly, he prepared to go over to the offensive with an all-out assault on the flank Hampton had found dangling. Sidling Early's men southward to fill the gap, Lee withdrew two of Hill's divisions from the trenches that evening and massed them south of the plank road, in the woods beyond the vulnerable enemy left, with orders to at-tack at dawn. Early would hold the fortified line overlooking Mine Run, while Hill drove the blue mass northward across his front and into the icy toils of the Rapidan. This time there would be no escape for Meade, as there had been for Hooker back in May, for there would be twelve solid hours of daylight for press-ing the attack, not a bare two or three, as there had been when Jackson struck in the late afternoon, under circumstances otherwise much the same.

★

"With God's blessing," the young staffer had predicted six nights ago, "there shall be a Second Chancellorsville." But he was wrong; God's blessing was withheld. When the flankers went forward at first light they found the thickets empty, the Federals gone. Chagrined (for though he had inflicted 1653 casualties at a cost of 629 — which brought the total of his losses to 4255 since Gettysburg, as compared to Meade's 4406 — he had counted on a stunning victory, defensive or offensive), Lee ordered his cavalry after them and followed with the infantry, marching as best he could through woods the bluecoats had set afire in their wake. It was no use; Meade's head start had been substantial, and he was back across the Rapidan before he could be overtaken.

In the Confederate ranks there was extreme regret at the lost opportunity, which grew in estimation, as was usual in such cases, in direct ratio to its inaccessibility. Early and Hill came under heavy criticism for having allowed the enemy to steal away unnoticed. "We miss Jackson and Longstreet terribly," the same staff officer remarked. But Lee, as always, took the blame on his own shoulders: shoulders on which he now was feeling the weight of his nearly fifty-seven years. "I am too old to command this army," he said sadly. "We should never have permitted those people to get away."

Although Davis shared the deep regret that Meade had not been punished more severely for his temporary boldness, he did not agree with Lee as to where the blame for this deliverance should rest. Conferring with the general at Orange on the eve of the brief Mine Run campaign, two weeks after his return from the roundabout western journey — it was the Commander in Chief's first visit to the Army of Northern Virginia since its departure from Richmond, nearly sixteen months before, to accomplish the suppression of Pope on the plains of Manassas — he had not failed to note the signs that Lee was aging, which indeed were unmistakable, but mainly he was impressed anew by his clear grasp of the tactical situation, his undiminished aggressiveness in the face of heavy odds, and the evident devotion of the veterans in his charge. Davis's admiration for this first of his field generals — especially by contrast with what he had observed in the course of his recent visit to the Army of Tennessee — was as strong as it had been four months ago, when he listed his reasons for refusing to accept Lee's suggestion that he be replaced as a corrective for the Gettysburg defeat.

By now though, as a result of what had happened around Chattanooga the week before, he had it once again in mind to shift him to new fields. Directed to take over from Bragg, who was relieved on the day Meade began his withdrawal from the Wilderness, Hardee replied as he had done when offered the command two months ago. He appreciated "this expression of [the President's] confidence," he said, "but feeling my inability to serve the country successfully in this new sphere of duty, I respectfully decline the command if designed to be permanent." Davis then turned, as he had turned before, to Lee: with similar results. The Virginian replied that he would of course go to North Georgia, if ordered, but "I have not that confidence either in my strength or ability as would lead me of my own option to undertake the command in question."

It was Lee's opinion that Beauregard was the logical choice for the post he had vacated a year and a half ago; but Davis liked this no better than he did the notion, advanced by others, that Johnston was the best man for the job. He had small use for either candidate. Deferring action on the matter until he had had a chance to talk it over with Lee in person, he wired for him to come to Richmond as soon as possible. Meantime the Chief Executive kept busy with affairs of state. Congress met for its fourth session on December 7, and the President's year-end message was delivered the following day.

"Gloom and unspoken despondency hang like a pall everywhere," a diarist noted on that date, adding: "Patriotism is a pretty heavy load to carry sometimes." Davis no doubt found it so on this occasion, obliged as he was to render a public account of matters better left unreviewed, since they could only thicken the gloom and add to the despondency they had provoked in the first place. In any case he made no attempt to minimize the defeats of the past fall and summer. Congress had adjourned in May; "Grave reverses befell our arms soon after your departure," he admitted at the outset. Charleston and Galveston were gleams in the prevailing murk, but they could scarcely relieve the fuliginous shadows thrown by Gettysburg and Vicksburg, along with other setbacks in that season of defeat, and the bright flame of Chickamauga had been damped by Missionary Ridge, which he confessed had been lost as the result of "misconduct by the troops."

So it went, throughout the reading of the lengthy message. Gains had been slight, losses heavy. Nor did Davis hold out hope of foreign intervention, as he had done so often in the past. Diplomatically, with recognition still withheld by the great powers beyond the Atlantic, the Confederacy was about as near the end of its rope as it was financially, with $600,000,000 in paper — "more than threefold the amount required by the business of the country" — already issued by the Treasury on little better security than a vague promise, which in turn was dependent on the outcome of a war it seemed to be losing. He could only propose the forcible reduction of the volume of currency; which in itself, as a later observer remarked, amounted to "a confession of bankruptcy." The end of the contest was nowhere in sight, he told the assembled legislators, and he recommended a tightening and extension of conscription as a

★

means of opposing the long numerical odds the Federals enjoyed. "We now know that the only reliable hope for peace is the vigor of our resistance," he declared, "while the cessation of their hostility is only to be expected from the pressure of their necessities."

In closing he came back to the South's chief asset, which had won for her the sometimes grudging admiration of the world. "The patriotism of the people has proved equal to every sacrifice demanded by their country's need. We have been united as a people never were united under like circumstances before. God has blessed us with success disproportionate to our means, and under His divine favor our labors must at last be crowned with the reward due to men who have given all they possessed to the righteous defense of their inalienable rights, their homes, and their altars."

★ ★ ★ *L*incoln's year-end message to the Federal Congress, which also convened on the first Monday in December, was delivered that same Tuesday, thus affording the people of the two nations, as well as those of the world at large, another opportunity for comparing the manner and substance of what the two leaders had to say in addressing themselves to events and issues which they viewed simultaneously from opposite directions. The resultant contrast was quite as emphatic as might have been expected, given their two positions and their two natures. Not only was there the obvious difference that what were admitted on one hand as defeats were announced as victories on the other, but there was also a considerable difference in tone. While Davis, referring defiantly to "the impassable gulf which divides us," denounced the "barbarous policy" and "savage ferocity" of an adversary "hardened in crime," the northern President spoke of reconciliation and advanced suggestions for coping with certain edgy problems that would loom when bloodshed ended. He dealt only in passing with specific military triumphs, recommending the annual reports of Stanton and Halleck as "documents of great interest," and contented himself with calling attention to the vast improvement of conditions in that regard since his last State of the Union address, just one week more than a year ago today. At that time, "amid much that was cold and menacing," he reminded the legislators, "the kindest words coming from Europe were uttered in accents of pity that we were too blind to surrender a hopeless cause"; whereas now, he pointed out, "the rebel borders are pressed still further back, and by the opening of the Mississippi the country dominated by the rebellion is divided into distinct parts, with no practical communication between them."

A share of the credit for this accomplishment was due to the Negro for his response to emancipation, Lincoln believed. "Of those who were slaves at the beginning of the rebellion, full one hundred thousand are now in the

Two black soldiers pose for the camera after enlisting in the Federal Army. By August 1863, the Union could boast of fourteen black regiments and twenty-four more in the process of formation.

United States military service, about one half of which number actually bear arms in the ranks; thus giving the double advantage of taking so much labor from the insurgent cause, and supplying the places which otherwise must be filled with so many white men. So far as tested, it is difficult to say they are not as good soldiers as any."

Having said so much, and reviewed as well such divergent topics as the budget, foreign relations, immigration, the homestead law, and Indian affairs, he passed at once to the main burden of his message, contained in an appended document titled "A Proclamation of Amnesty and Reconstruction." Lately, in answer to a letter in which Zachariah Chandler, pleased by the outcome of the fall elections but alarmed by reports that the moderates were urging their views on the President during the preparation of this report on the State of the Union, had warned him to "stand firm" against such influences and pressures — "Conservatives and traitors are buried together," the Michigan senator told him; "for God's sake don't exhume their remains in your Message. They will smell worse than Lazarus did after he had been buried three days" — Lincoln had sought to calm the millionaire dry goods merchant's fears. "I am

★

glad the elections this autumn have gone favorably," he replied, "and that I have not, by native depravity, or under evil influences, done anything bad enough to prevent the good result. I hope to 'stand fast' enough not to go backward, and yet not to go forward fast enough to wreck the country's cause."

The appended document, setting forth his views on amnesty for individuals and reconstruction of the divided nation, was an example of what he meant. In essence, it provided that all Confederates — with certain specified exceptions, such as holders of public office, army generals and naval officers above the rank of lieutenant, former U.S. congressmen and judges, and anyone found guilty of mistreating prisoners of war — would receive a full executive pardon upon taking an oath of loyalty to the federal government, support of the Emancipation Proclamation, and obedience to all lawful acts in reference to slavery. Moreover, as soon as one tenth of the 1860 voters in any seceded state had taken the oath prescribed, that state would be readmitted to the Union and the enjoyment of its constitutional rights, including representation in Congress.

Reactions varied, but whether its critics thought the proclamation outrageous or sagacious, a further example of wheedling or a true gesture of magnanimity, there were the usual objections to the message as proof of Lincoln's ineptness whenever he tried to come to grips with the English language. "Its words and sentences fall in heaps, instead of flowing in a connected stream, and it is therefore difficult reading," the *Journal of Commerce* pointed out, while the Chicago *Times* was glibly scornful of the backwoods President's lack of polish. "Slipshod as have been all his literary performances," the Illinois editor complained, "this is the most slovenly of all. If they were slipshod, this is barefoot, and the feet, plainly enough, never have been shod." However, the *New York Times* found the composition "simple and yet perfectly effective," and Horace Greeley was even more admiring. He thought the proclamation "devilish good," and predicted that it would "break the back of the Rebellion," though he stopped well short of the *Tribune*'s White House correspondent's judgment that "no President's message since George Washington retired into private life has given such general satisfaction as that sent to Congress by Abraham Lincoln today."

Just how general that satisfaction might be, he did not say, but one person in emphatic disagreement was Charles Sumner, who, as he sat listening to the drone of the clerk at the joint session, favored visitors and colleagues with a demonstration of the inefficacy of caning as a corrective for infantile behavior. Watching as he "gave vent to his half-concealed anger," a journalist observed that, "during the delivery of the Message, the distinguished Senator from Massachusetts exhibited his petulance to the galleries by eccentric motions in his chair, pitching his documents and books upon the floor in ill-tempered disgust."

Sumner's disgust with this plan for reconstruction was based in part on his agreement with the New York *Herald* editor who, commenting on the proposal that ten percent of the South's voters be allowed to return the region to the Union, stated flatly that he did not believe there were "that many good men there." Besides, the Bay State senator had his own notion of the way to deal with traitors, and it was nothing at all like Lincoln's. In a recent issue of the *Atlantic Monthly* he had advocated the division of the Confederacy, as soon as it had been brought to its knees, into eleven military districts under eleven imported governors, "all receiving their authority from one source, ruling a population amounting to upward of nine millions. And this imperial domain, indefinite in extent, will also be indefinite in duration . . . with all powers, executive, legislative, and even judicial, derived from one man in Washington." Although he admitted that "in undertaking to create military governors, we reverse the policy of the Republic as solemnly declared by Jefferson, and subject the civil to the military authority," he thought such treatment no worse than was deserved by cane-swinging hotheads who had brought on the war by their pretense of secession. So far as he was concerned, though he continued to deny the right of secession, he was willing to accept it as an act of political suicide. Those eleven states were indeed out of the Union, and the victors had the right to do with them as they chose, including their resettlement with good Republican voters and the determination of when and under what conditions they were to be readmitted. Most of the members of his party agreed, foreseeing a solid Republican South.

Lincoln wanted that too, of course, but he did not believe that this was the best way to go about securing it. For one thing, such an arrangement was likely to last no longer than it took the South to get back on its feet. For another, he wanted those votes now, or at any rate in time for next year's presidential and congressional elections, not at the end of some period "indefinite in duration." Therefore he considered it "vain and profitless" to speculate on whether the rebellious states had withdrawn or could withdraw from the Union, even though this was precisely the issue on which most people thought the war was being fought. "We know that they were and we trust that they shall be in the Union," he said. "It does not greatly matter whether in the meantime they shall be considered to have been in or out."

This was a rift that would widen down the years, but for the present the Jacobins kept their objections within bounds, knowing well enough that when readmission time came round, it would be Congress that would sit in judgment on the applicants. Southward, however, the reaction was both violent and sudden. Lincoln's ruthlessness — an element of his political genius that was to receive small recognition from posthumous friends who were safe beyond his reach — had long been apparent to his foes. For example, in addition to the unkept guarantees he had given slaveholders in his inaugural address, he had declared on revoking Frémont's emancipation order that such matters "must be settled according to laws made by law-makers, and not by military proclamations," and he had classified as "simply 'dictatorship' " any government "wherein a general, or a President, may make permanent rules of property by proclamation." Thus he had written in late September of the first year of the war, exactly one year before he issued his own preliminary emancipation proclamation, which differed from Frémont's only in scope, being also military, and which showed him to be a man who would hold to principles only so long as he had more to gain than lose by them. Observing this, Confederates defined him as slippery, mendacious, and above all not to be trusted.

Certainly Davis saw him in that light, increasingly so with the passing months, and never more so than in this early-December amnesty offer. "That despot," he now called Lincoln, whose "purpose in his message and proclamation was to shut out all hope that he would *ever* treat with us, on *any* terms." Acceptance would amount to unconditional surrender, Davis asserted, and by way of showing what he meant he paraphrased the offer: "If we will break up our government, dissolve the Confederacy, disband our armies, emancipate our slaves, take an oath of allegiance binding ourselves to him and to disloyalty to our states, he proposes to pardon us and not to plunder us of anything more than the property already stolen from us. . . . In order to render his proposals so insulting as to secure their rejection, he joins to them a promise to support with his army one tenth of the people of any state who will attempt to set up a government over the other nine tenths, thus seeking to sow discord and suspicion among the people of the several states, and to excite them to civil war in furtherance of his ends."

Thus Davis reflected a reversed mirror-image of his adversary's offer, saying: "I do not believe that the vilest wretch would accept such terms." Without exception southern editors agreed. "We who have committed no offense need no forgiveness," they protested, quoting Benjamin Franklin's reply to a British offer of amnesty. "How impudent it is," the Richmond *Sentinel* observed of Lincoln, "to come with our brothers' blood upon his accursed hands, and ask us to accept his forgiveness! But he goes further. He makes his forgiveness dependent on terms." Congress was more vigorous in its protest. Resolutions were introduced denouncing "the truly characteristic proclamation of amnesty issued by the imbecile and unprincipled usurper who now sits enthroned upon the ruins of Constitutional liberty in Washington City," while others made it abundantly clear that the people of the Confederacy, through their elected representatives, did "hereby, solemnly and irrevocably, utterly deny, defy, spurn back, and scorn the terms of amnesty offered by Abraham Lincoln in his official proclamation." All such resolutions were tabled, however, upon the protest by one member that they "would appear to dignify a paper emanating from that wretched and detestable abortion, whose contemptible emptiness and folly will only receive the ridicule of the civilized world." It was decided, accordingly, that "the true and only treatment which that miserable and contemptible despot, Lincoln, should receive at the hands of the House is silent and unmitigated contempt."

Unmitigated this contempt might be, but silent was the one thing it was not. In fact, as various members continued to plumb and scale the various depths and heights of oratory, it grew more strident all the time. Evidently they had been touched where they were sore. And indeed, in its review of Lincoln's message, the New York *World* had warned that such would be the case. Violence was a characteristic of the revolutionary impulse, the *World* declared; "You can no more control it than a flaxen hand can fetter flame"; so that if what the President was really seeking was reconciliation — or even, as Davis claimed, division within the Confederate ranks — he could scarcely have chosen a worse approach. "If Mr Lincoln were a statesman, if he were even a man of ordinary prudence and sagacity, he would see the necessity for touching the peculiar wound of the South with as light a hand as possible." What the editor had in mind was slavery, and so did the frock-coated gentlemen in Richmond, along with much else which they believed was endangered by this war of arms and propaganda. In the course of their two-month session they gave the matter a great deal of attention, and before it was over they produced a joint resolution, issued broadcast as an "Address of Congress to the People of the Confederate States." Specifically an attack on the Lincoln administration for its policies and conduct of the war, the resolution was also an exhortation for the southern people to continue their resistance to northern force and blandishments, including the recent amnesty proclamation.

It is absurd to pretend that a government really desirous of restoring the Union would adopt such measures as the confiscation of private property, the emancipation of slaves, the division of a sovereign state without its consent, and a proclamation that one tenth of the population of a state, and that tenth under military rule, should control the will of the remaining nine tenths. The only relation possible between the two sections under such a policy is that of conqueror and conquered, superior and dependent. Rest assured, fellow citizens, that although restoration may still be used as a war cry by the northern government, it is only to delude and betray.

★

Fanaticism has summoned to its aid cupidity and vengeance, and nothing short of your utter subjugation, the destruction of your state governments, the overthrow of your social and political fabric, your personal and public degradation and ruin, will satisfy the demands of the North.

About midway through the lengthy document, after charging that the Federals had provoked the war and were "accountable for the blood and havoc and ruin it has caused," the legislators presented a catalogue of "atrocities too incredible for narration."

Instead of a regular war, our resistance to the unholy efforts to crush out our national existence is treated as a rebellion, and the settled international rules between belligerents are ignored. Instead of conducting the war as betwixt two military and political organizations, it is a war against the whole population. Houses are pillaged and burned. Churches are defaced. Towns are ransacked. Clothing of women and infants is stripped from their persons. Jewelry and mementoes of the dead are stolen. Mills and implements of agriculture are destroyed. Private saltworks are broken up. The introduction of medicines is forbidden. Means of subsistence are wantonly wasted to produce beggary. Prisoners are returned with contagious diseases. . . .

The list continued, then finally broke off. "We tire of these indignities and enormities. They are too sickening for recital," the authors confessed, and passed at once to the lesson to be learned from them. "It is better to be conquered by any other nation than by the United States. It is better to be a dependency of any other power than of that. . . . We cannot afford to take steps backward. Retreat is more dangerous than advance. Behind us are inferiority and degradation. Before us is everything enticing to a patriot." As for how the war was to be won, the answer was quite simple: by perseverance.

★

Moral like physical epidemics have their allotted periods, and must sooner or later be exhausted and disappear. When reason returns, our enemies will probably reflect that a people like ours, who have exhibited such capabilities and extemporized such resources, can never be subdued; that a vast expanse of territory with such a population cannot be governed as an obedient colony. Victory would not be conquest. The inextinguishable quarrel would be transmitted "from bleeding sire to son," and the struggle would be renewed between generations yet unborn. . . . There is no just reason for hopelessness or fear. Since the outbreak of the war the South has lost the nominal possession of the Mississippi River and fragments of her territory; but Federal occupation is not conquest. The fires of patriotism still burn unquenchably in the breasts of those who are subject to foreign domination. We have yet in our uninterrupted control a territory which, according to past progress, will require the enemy ten years to overrun.

In conclusion — though the words came strangely from the lips of men who, despite their nominal membership in a single national party, comprised perhaps the most fractious, factious political assembly in the western world to date — the legislators recommended "unfaltering trust," on the part of the southern people in their leaders, as the surest guide if they would tread "the path that leads to honor and peace, although it lead through tears and suffering and blood."

Let all spirit of faction and past party differences be forgotten in the presence of our cruel foe. . . . We entreat from all a generous and hearty coöperation with the government in all branches of its administration, and with the agents, civil or military, in the performance of their duties. Moral aid has the "power of the incommunicable," and, by united efforts, by an

all-comprehending and self-sacrificing patriotism, we can,

with the blessing of God, avert the perils which environ us,

and achieve for ourselves and children peace and freedom.

Hitherto the Lord has interposed graciously to bring us victo-

ry, and in His hand there is present power to prevent this

great multitude which come against us from casting us out of

the possession which He has given us to inherit.

Such were the first bitter fruits of Lincoln's proclamation, offering amnesty to individuals and seeking to establish certain guidelines for the future reconstruction of the South.

★ ★ ★ **R**eceiving on December 9 the President's instructions for him to come to Richmond, Lee supposed a decision had been reached to send him to North Georgia as Bragg's successor, despite his expressed reluctance to leave the Old Dominion and the army whose fame had grown with his own in the eighteen months since Davis placed him at its head. With Longstreet in East Tennessee, Ewell absent sick, and A. P. Hill as usual in poor health, the summons came at what seemed to him an unfortunate time, particularly since the latter two, even aside from their physical debility, had not fulfilled his expectations in their present subordinate positions. But orders were orders; he left at once. "My heart and thoughts will always be with this army," he said in a note to Stuart as he boarded at Orange a train that had him in the capital before nightfall.

He found to his relief, however, that no decision had been made regarding his transfer to the western theater. The President, in conference with his Cabinet on the matter of selecting a new leader for the army temporarily under Hardee, had merely wanted his ranking field commander there to share in the discussion. Lee's reluctance having been honored to the extent that it had removed him from consideration for the post, the advisers found it difficult to agree on a second choice. Not only were they divided among themselves; Davis withheld approval of every candidate proposed. Some were all for Beauregard, for instance, but the Commander in Chief had even less confidence in the Creole than he had in Joe Johnston, who was being recommended warmly in the press, on the floor of Congress, in letters from friends, and by Seddon. While the Secretary admitted that he had been disappointed by his fellow Virginian's "absence of enterprise" in the recent Mississippi operations, he believed that "his military sagacity would not fail to recognize the exigencies of the time and position, and so direct all his thoughts and skill to an offensive campaign." Davis was doubtful. He rather agreed with Benjamin, who protested that during his six-month tenure as Secretary of War he had found in Johnston "tendencies to defensive strategy and a lack of knowledge of the environment." Others present inclined to the same view. On the evidence, Old Joe's talent seemed primarily for retreat: so much so, indeed, that if left to his own devices he might be expected to wind up gingerly defending Key West and complaining that he lacked transportation for a withdrawal to Cuba in the event that something threatened one of his flanks.

Finally, however, at the close of a full week of discussion, Johnston was favored by a majority of those present, and the minority, though still unreconciled to his appointment, confessed that it had no one else to offer. According to Seddon, "the President, after doubt and with misgiving to the end, chose him . . . not as with exaltation on this score, but as the best on the whole to be obtained." He wired him at Meridian that same day, December 16, two weeks after Bragg had been relieved: "You will turn over the immediate command of the Army of Mississippi to Lieutenant General Polk and proceed to Dalton and assume command of the Army of Tennessee. . . . A letter of instructions will be sent to you at Dalton."

Requested to inspect the capital defenses, Lee stayed on for another five days, during which time he was lionized by the public and invited by the House of Representatives to take what was infelicitously called "a seat on the floor." After the Sunday service at Saint Paul's he was given a silent ovation as he passed down the aisle, bowing left and right to friends in the congregation, and forty-year-old Mrs Chesnut, who prided herself on her sophistication, confessed in her diary that when the general "bowed low and gave me a smile of recognition, I was ashamed of being so pleased. I blushed like a schoolgirl."

A four-day extension of the visit would have allowed him to spend his first Christmas with his family since two years before the war, but he would not have it so; he was thinking of his army on the Rapidan and the men there who were far from home as this gayest of holidays drew near. For their part, while they envied, they did not resent his good fortune. In point of fact, they doubted that he would take advantage of it. "It will be more in accordance with his peculiar character," a staff major wrote from Orange to his sweetheart on December 20, "if he leaves for the army just before the great anniversary; he is so very apt to suppress or deny his personal desire when it conflicts with the performance of his duty." The young officer was right. Lee returned next day, having sacrificed a Richmond Christmas with his wife in order to be with his troops and share in their frugal celebration of what had always been for Southerners a combination of all that was best in the gladdest days of the departing year.

All was quiet in the camps along the Rapidan, but the cavalry had been kept busy in his absence — and fruitlessly busy, at that — attempting to head off or break up a raid into Southwest Virginia, deep in the army's rear, by a column of hard-riding horsemen under Averell, who had been given an independent brigade after Hooker relieved him of duty amid the fury of Chancellorsville. Regaining the safety of his own lines on the day Lee returned to Orange, Averell proudly reported that in the past two weeks his troopers had "marched, climbed, slid, and swum 355 miles," avoided superior combinations of graybacks sent to scatter or capture them, and cut the Tennessee & Virginia Railroad at Salem (just west of a hamlet called Big Lick, which twenty years later would change its name to Roanoke and grow to be a city) where three depots crammed with food and equipment on consignment to the Army of Northern Virginia were set afire. At a cost of 6 men drowned, 5 wounded, and 94 missing, he had captured some 200 of the enemy, 84 of whom he brought back with him, together with about 150 horses. This time he left no sack of coffee for his friend Fitzhugh Lee, who commanded one of the columns that faile d to intercept him, but he could say, as he had said before: "Here's your visit. How do you like it?" Fitz liked it no better

Mary Custis Lee smiles serenely in this prewar portrait. Later, crippling arthritis and loneliness caused by her husband's long absences during the Mexican and Civil Wars took their toll on her.

now than he had done in March, after Kelly's Ford. Nor did Stuart, who was presented with further evidence of the decline of the advantage he had enjoyed in the
days when his superior riders were mounted on superior, well-fed horses.

Meanwhile the foot soldiers took it easy, blue and gray alike. Meade's
withdrawal from Lee's formidable Mine Run front — accomplished with such
skill and stealth that his opponent's resultant attitude resembled that of a greenhorn lured into the Wilderness by pranksters who left him holding the bag on a
"snipe hunt" — had ended all infantry operations for the year. On both sides of
the river the two armies went into winter quarters, beginning what would be a
five-month rest. On the north bank, for Meade despite his crankiness was liberal
in such matters, generals, colonels, majors, even captains were able to bring their
wives into camp on extended visits. One witness considered their presence greatly
beneficial, and not only to their husbands. "Their influence softens and human-
izes much that might otherwise be harsh and repulsive," he declared. "In their
company, at least, officers who should be gentlemen do not get drunk." On the
other hand, a high-toned Massachusetts staff man was a good deal less enthusiastic about these army ladies. "Such a set of feminine humans I have not seen often," he wrote home. "It was Lowell's factories broken loose and gone wild."

However, except on the off chance that a few orderlies got lucky, all
this meant little to the enlisted men, who were obliged to depend on their own
resources and limit the count of their blessings to the fact that they were not to
be shot at for a while. "The troops burrowed into the earth and built their little
shelters," a Federal brigadier was to recall, "and the officers and men devoted
themselves to unlimited festivity, balls, horse races, cockfights, greased pigs and
poles, and other games such as only soldiers can devise."

★ ★ ★ **F**or most of the people of Richmond, women and old
men and children, politicians and officeholders of high
and low degree, as well as for the maimed and convalescent
veterans in private homes and hospitals on the city's seven hills, this holiday
season was scarcely gayer than it was for their friends and kinsmen on the Rapidan with Lee. For some few others, however, owners of plantations down the
country, not yet taken over by invaders, provisions had been forwarded for laying out a meal that had at least a resemblance to the feasts of olden times.
Christmas dinner at Colonel and Mrs Chesnut's, for example, included oyster
soup, boiled mutton, ham, boned turkey, wild duck and partridges, plum pud-
ding, and four kinds of wine to wash it down with. "There is life in the old
land yet!" the diarist exclaimed.

Among her guests that day was John Bell Hood, the social catch of
the town. Taken a few miles south of the field where he lost his leg, he had spent
a month in bed on a North Georgia farm and then, because it was feared he

★

might be captured so near the enemy lines, continued his convalescence in Atlanta for another month before coming on to Richmond in late November. With his left arm still in a sling and his right trouser leg hanging empty, his eyes deep-set in a pain-gaunted face above the full blond beard of a Wagnerian hero, the thirty-two-year-old bachelor general had the ladies fluttering around him, his hostess said, "as if it would be a luxury to pull out their handkerchiefs and have a good cry." Instead, they brought him oranges and peeled and sliced them for him, prompting another guest to remark that "the money value of friendship is easily counted now," since oranges were selling in the capital markets for five Confederate dollars each. Shortly after Chickamauga, Longstreet had recommended the Kentucky-born Texan's promotion to lieutenant general "for distinguished conduct and ability in the battle of the 20th instant." Moreover, although Hood was nearly six years younger than A. P. Hill, the present youngest officer of that rank, there was little doubt that the promotion would be confirmed; for he was now an intimate of the President's and accompanied him on carriage rides and tours of inspection, in and about the city.

Another Kentuckian was being talked about on all sides this Christmas, here and elsewhere, and did much to lift the gloom resulting from the reverses lately suffered, including his own. On November 28 word flashed across the North and South that John Morgan and six of his captains, taken with him in the course of the raid that ended near Salineville four months back, had escaped the night before from the Ohio Penitentiary by tunneling out of their cell block and scaling the outer wall. That was all that was known for the time being, except that Buckeye posses bent on his recapture were combing the region and searching the cellars and attics of all suspected Copperheads. In mid-December, two weeks later, he turned up on the near bank of the Tennessee River, below Kingston, and soon afterwards crossed the Great Smoky Mountains to Franklin, North Carolina, well beyond reach of the searchers in his rear.

The particulars of his flight were as daring as the wildest of his raids. Dressed as civilians, he and his companions had boarded a fast night express at Columbus, just outside the prison walls, and reached Cincinnati before the morning bed check showed them missing from their cells. By that time they were over the Ohio, riding south on borrowed horses — there was little in the Bluegrass that John Morgan could not have for the asking — to cross the Cumberland near Burkesville. Two of the party had been lost just outside Louisville, picked up by a Federal patrol, but the others made it all the way. Morgan himself reached Danville, Virginia, in time for Christmas dinner with his wife, who was recuperating there from a miscarriage, brought on it was said by worry about her husband and resentment of Ohio's vindictive treatment of him as a felon. Now he was with her again, and soon he would be back with the army, too. He had been summoned to Richmond, where a public reception was being planned in his honor, he was informed, "thusly [to] say to the despicable foe that in their futile efforts to degrade you before the world they have only elevated you in the estimation of all Confederate citizens, and the whole civilized world."

Anticipation of his arrival, which was scheduled for January 2, gave a lift to the spirits of the people of the capital. But for many, unable to draw on such resources as were available to the Chesnuts and their guests, the holiday itself was depressing in its contrast to the ones they had enjoyed last year and the year before, when the festivities were heightened by recent victories at Fredericksburg and Ball's Bluff. No such occasions warranted celebration now. "It is a sad, cold Christmas, and threatening snow," a government clerk recorded in his diary. "The children have a Christmas tree, but it is not burdened. Candy is held at $8 per pound." Nor did he find much evidence of merriment among his fellow townsmen when he went out for a walk that afternoon. "Occasionally an *exempt,* who has speculated, may be seen drunk. But a somber heaviness is in the countenances of men as well as in the sky above." Although, like candy, a Christmas turkey was beyond his means, "[I] do not covet one. This is no time for feasting," he declared. Presently, if only out of surfeit, Mrs Chesnut was inclined to agree. "God help my country!" she exclaimed on New Year's Day, looking back somewhat ruefully on the round of holiday parties she had given or attended. "I think we are like the sailors who break into the spirits closet when they find out the ship must sink."

Reviewing her correspondence for the year now past, she came upon an early draft of a letter she had written Varina Davis during a September visit to the South Carolina plantation that furnished so many delicacies for her table. It had seemed to her then, she told the first lady, that the people were divided into two main groups, one made up of enthusiasts whose "whole duty here consists of abusing Lincoln and the Yankees, praising Jeff Davis and the army of Virginia, and wondering when this horrid war will be over," while the other included "politicians and men with no stomach for fighting, who find it easier to cuss Jeff Davis and stay at home than to go to the front with a musket. They are the kind who came out almost as soon as they went into the war, dissatisfied with the way things were managed. Joe Johnston is their polar star, the redeemer!"

Polar star and redeemer he might be to the disaffected Carolinians, as well as to the western soldiers once more in his charge, but to his superiors in Richmond he was something else again. Receiving the President's telegram of December 16, the general spent a few days putting his affairs in order, including the transfer of his present command to Polk, and then on December 22 set out by rail for North Georgia. Two days after Christmas he reached Dalton, where he took over from Hardee without further delay.

Awaiting him there were the instructions promised in the wire received ten days ago in Mississippi, one set from the Commander in Chief and

Mary Chesnut, wife of a Confederate officer and aide to Jefferson Davis, moved in the highest society of Charleston. She kept a journal of her daily life from February 1861 until after Appomattox.

another from the Secretary of War, both urging an early campaign against the Federals in his front. While admitting that "the army may have been, by recent events, somewhat disheartened," Seddon believed that Johnston's presence would restore its "discipline, prestige, and confidence" in preparation for the recovery of all that had been lost. "As soon as the condition of your forces will allow," the Secretary added, "it is hoped that you will be able to assume the offensive." Davis wrote in a similar vein. Information lately received encouraged "a not unfavorable view of the material of the command," he said, and "induces me to hope that you will soon be able to commence active operations against the enemy. . . . You will not need to have it suggested that the imperative demand for prompt and vigorous action arises not only from the importance of restoring the prestige of the army, and averting the dispiriting and injurious results that must attend a season of inactivity, but also from the necessity of re-occupying the country upon the supplies of which the proper subsistence of the armies materially depends." The general on the scene could best determine "the immediate measures to be adopted in attaining this end," the President remarked, and he urged him to "communicate fully and freely with me concerning your proposed plan of action, that all the assistance and co-operation may be most advantageously afforded that it is in the power of the government to render. Trusting that your health may be preserved, and that the arduous and responsible duties you have undertaken may be successfully accomplished, I remain very respectfully and truly yours, Jeffn Davis."

Whereupon — in response to these conciliatory statements of confidence in the general's ability, these offers to replace past bitterness with cordiality — the old trouble rose anew, bringing with it apparent confirmation of the doubts expressed by Benjamin and others at the series of high-level conferences leading to the choice of a new commander for the Army of Tennessee. Johnston had not thought he would get the post; "The temper exhibited toward me makes it very unlikely that I shall ever again occupy an important position," he told a friend in mid-September; but when he learned of his new assignment, three months later, he was delighted. This reaction lasted no longer, however, than it took him to reach Dalton and read the letters of instruction. As always, he bridled at what he considered prodding, especially from these two, who all through June had tried to persuade him to wreck his army for no purpose, so far as he could see, except as a gesture of sympathy for the garrison penned up in Vicksburg as a result of their unwisdom. Now here they were, at it again, trying to nudge him into rashness and disaster!

His reply to Seddon was edged with irony. "The duties of military administration you point out to me shall be attended to with diligence," he said. But he added flatly: "This army is now far from being in condition to 'resume the offensive.' " A similar reply went to Davis. "Your Excellency well impresses upon me the importance of recovering the territory we have lost. I feel it deeply; but difficulties appear to me in the way." These he listed in considerable detail, including a shortage of transportation and subsistence, the long numerical odds the Federals enjoyed, and the poor condition of the roads because of recent heavy rains. He might be able to resist an attack in his present position, he declared, but under the conditions now prevailing he could not even entertain the notion of delivering one. In short: "I can see no other mode of taking the offensive here than to beat the enemy when he advances, and then move forward."

There they had it — as, indeed, they had had it so often before, wherever Johnston commanded in this war. The Manassas region beyond the Rappahannock, the York-James peninsula, the Mississippi heartland, all had been given up by him on the heels of similar protests at suggestions that he "assume the offensive" or merely stand his ground. Seddon and Davis saw their worst fears realized. If past performance was any indication of what to expect, Johnston would backpedal in response to whatever pressure the enemy brought against him in North Georgia, and this time it would be the *national* heartland that would pass into Federal possession as a result. Their inclination was to remove him before that happened, but this would mean a return to the problem of finding another commander for the army, which was no more soluble now than it had been in mid-December. They had him; they would have to live with him. The result, as they continued to plead for an advance and he continued to bridle at the prodding, was increased dissatisfaction and petulance at both ends of the telegraph wires connecting Richmond and Dalton.

Whatever second thoughts his superiors might be having as to their wisdom in appointing this new commander of the Army of Tennessee, the men under him were delighted. In fact, the pleasure they had experienced on hearing of Bragg's departure was redoubled by the news that Johnston was to take his place, and according to one veteran's recollection, civilians reacted in a similar manner: "At every bivouac in the field, at every fireside in the rear, the joyous dawn of day seemed to have arisen from the night." Rations improved with the Virginian's arrival; the clothing issue was liberalized; even a system of furloughs was established. Moreover, whereas Bragg had kept to his tent between campaigns — confined there, more often than not, by dyspepsia — Johnston not only made it a point to pay frequent visits to all the camps, he also did not limit his attention to men with bars or stars on their collars. "He passed through the ranks of the common soldiers, shaking hands with every one he met," a private was to recall years later. "He restored the soldier's pride; he brought the manhood back to the private's bosom; he changed the order of roll-call, standing guard, drill, and such nonsense as that. The revolution was complete. He was loved, respected, admired; yea, almost worshipped by his troops. I do not believe there was a soldier in his army but would gladly have died for him."

This last was based in part no doubt on their knowledge that he would ask of them no dying he could spare them; that he believed, as they did, in a minimum of bloodshed, and would always sacrifice mere terrain if the price of holding it seemed to him excessive. But there was a good deal more to it than that. Veneration was deepened by affection, and the affection was returned. No matter how touchy Johnston might be in his relations with superiors, he was invariably friendly to those below him on the military ladder, considerate of their needs and never seeming to fear that this might lessen his dignity or cost him any measure of their respect.

One day soon after his arrival in Dalton, for example, Cheatham brought a number of men from his division over to army headquarters in a body, accompanied by a band with which to serenade the new commander. Presently Johnston stepped hatless from his tent to thank them for the music and the visit; whereupon Cheatham performed a highly informal ceremony of introduction. "Boys," he said, affectionately patting the general's bald head two or three times as he spoke, "this is Old Joe."

★　★　★

★

*A flag snaps in the sea breeze
as Federal officers pose in front of
the Hilton Head, South Carolina,
headquarters of Major General
Quincy A. Gillmore.*

T W O

Olustee; Kilpatrick Raid

1863 ★ ★ ★ ★ ★ In all seasons and all weathers, stifling heat or numbing cold, the men aboard the Federal blockaders kept their stations, stood their watches, and patrolled their designated segments of the highly irregular three thousand miles of coastline between Old Point Comfort and Matamoros. Not for them had been the thunderous runs by the frigates and gunboats under Farragut and Porter, during which the world seemed turned to flame and a man's heart pounded as if to break the confines of his ribs, or the exhilarating chases by the raiders under Semmes and Maffitt, staged hundreds of miles from the sight of land and punctuated with coaling stops in sinful foreign ports. A sailor who managed to secure a leave from one of the river fleets was sure to receive at home a hero's welcome for his share in the humbling of Vicksburg or Port Hudson, and since her sinking of the *Hatteras,* off Galveston a year ago, the *Alabama* had added an even three dozen Yankee ships and barks and schooners to her string of prizes, while the *Florida,* after her nimble sprint out of Mobile Bay, had taken just over two dozen such merchant vessels in that same span. The men on blockade duty envied blue and gray alike, not only for the stormy present but also for the future still to come. Someday perhaps, if they survived the boredom and saltpeter, there would be the question: "What did you do, Father, in the war?" Within the limitations of

★

the truth, about the only satisfactory answer they could give — satisfactory to themselves, that is — would be: "I'd rather not talk about it."

Nor were conditions any better in that regard for the crews of ships assigned to add offensive punch to the four blockading squadrons. In contrast to 1862, when it had appeared that no salt-water attack could fail, whatever the objective, the year just past had seen no fort subdued, no harbor seized, except along the scantly defended lower coast of Texas, where the year-end gains were far outweighed by the reverses suffered earlier at Galveston and Sabine Pass. If such efforts on the Gulf amounted to little, those on the Atlantic came to less. Du Pont's repulse at Charleston, and Dahlgren's protracted frustration since, had served no purpose the men could discern except to make them thankful that the brass had not seen fit to test the defenses of Wilmington or Mobile. There were dangers enough outside such places, it seemed to them, without venturing any closer: as the *Ironsides* could testify, having had her timbers shivered by the

---

Boredom was the main problem, especially for the crews of the blockaders, who could not see that their day-in day-out service had much to do with fighting at all . . .

---

unscathed *David*. Two months later, on December 6, the monitor *Weehawken* — leader of the nine-boat iron column that had steamed into Charleston harbor back in April — met a harsher and still more ignominious fate, without an enemy in sight. Tied up to a buoy inside the bar, she had taken on an extra load of heavy ammunition which so reduced her freeboard that the ebb tide flooded an open hawse pipe and a hatch, foundering her so rapidly that she carried 31 of her crew with her on her sudden plunge to the bottom. There was small glory here for either the dead or the survivors, who were promptly transferred to other vessels to keep up the work of raising puffs of brick dust from the defiant ruin of Sumter. Morale was not helped, either, when they learned of Father Gideon's response to a request from Dahlgren — who knew something of the strain on their nerves because of the jangled state of his own — that a whiskey ration be distributed under medical supervision. Welles did not approve. He recommended that iced coffee or oatmeal mixed with water be used as a pick-me-up instead.

Boredom was the main problem, especially for the crews of the blockaders, who could not see that their day-in day-out service had much to do with fighting at all, let alone with speeding the victory which hard-war politicians and editors kept saying was just around the corner. Off Cape Fear, where the sleek gray runners steaming in from Nassau and Bermuda found cover under the unchallenged guns of Fort Fisher, a bluejacket wrote home to his mother (as the letter was paraphrased years later by a student of the era) that she could get some notion of blockade duty if she would "go to the roof on a hot summer day, talk to a half dozen degenerates, descend to the basement, drink tepid water full of iron rust, climb to the roof again, and repeat the process at intervals until she was fagged out, then go to bed with everything shut tight." Individual reactions to this monotony, which was scarcely relieved by an unbroken diet of moldy beans, stale biscuits, and sour pork, varied from fisticuffs and insubordination to homosexuality and desertion. Officers fraternized ashore with Negro women, a practice frowned on by the Navy, and mess crews specialized in the manufacture of outlaw whiskey distilled from almost any substance that would ferment in the southern heat — as in fact nearly everything would, including men. Rheumatism and scurvy kept the doctors busy, along with breakbone fever, hemorrhoids, and damage done by knuckles. These they could deal with, after their fashion, but there was no medicine for the ills of the spirit, brought on by the strain of monotony, poor food, and unhealthy living conditions, which produced much longer casualty lists than did rebel shells or torpedoes. "Give me a discharge, and let me go home," a distraught but articulate coal heaver begged his skipper after months of duty outside Charleston. "I am a poor weak, miserable, nervous, half crazy boy. . . . Everything jars upon my delicate nerves."

Inside the harbor, Beauregard was about as deep in the doldrums as were the blue-clad sailors beyond the bar. Disappointed that he had not been ordered west to resume command of the army Bragg had inherited from him, privately he was telling friends that his usefulness in the war had ended, and he predicted defeat for the Confederacy no later than spring or summer. He gave as the cause for both of these disasters "the persistent inability and obstinacy of our rulers." Primarily he meant Davis, of whom he said: "The curse of God must have been on our people when we chose him out of so many noble sons of the South, who would have carried us safely through this Revolution."

In addition to the frustration proceeding from his belief that presidential animosity, as evidenced by slights and snubs, had cost him the western command he so much wanted, the Creole's gloom was also due to the apparent failure of a new weapon he had predicted would accomplish, unassisted, the lifting of the Union blockade by the simple process of sinking the blockaders. There had arrived by rail from Mobile in mid-August, disassembled and loaded on two flatcars, a cigar-shaped metal vessel about thirty feet in length and less than four feet wide and five feet deep. Put back together and launched in Charleston harbor, she resembled the little *David*-class torpedo boats whose low silhouette made them hard for enemy lookouts to detect. Actually, though, she had been designed to carry this advantage a considerable step further, in that

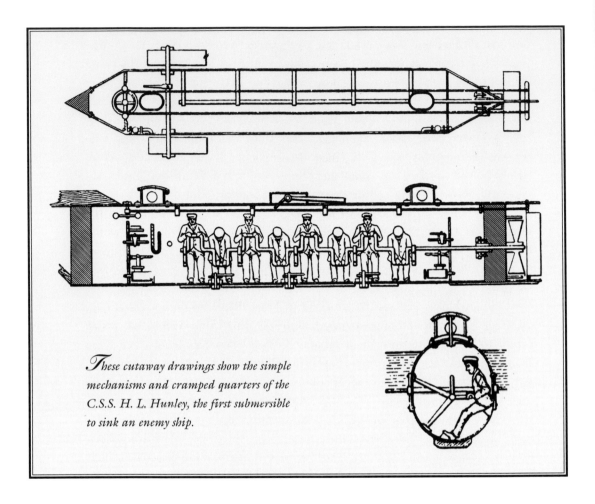

These cutaway drawings show the simple mechanisms and cramped quarters of the C.S.S. H. L. Hunley, the first submersible to sink an enemy ship.

she was intended to travel under as well as on the water, and thus present no silhouette at all. She was, in short, the world's first submarine.

Christened the *H. L. Hunley* for one of her builders, who had come from Alabama with her to instruct the Carolinians in her use, she was propeller-driven but had no engine, deriving her power from her eight-man crew, posted at cranks along her drive shaft, which they turned on orders from her coxswain-captain. Water was let into ballast tanks to lower her until she was nearly awash; then her two hatches were bolted tight from inside, and as she moved forward the skipper took her down by depressing a pair of horizontal fins, which were also used to level and raise her while in motion. To bring her all the way up, force pumps ejected the water from her tanks, decreasing her specific gravity; or in emergencies her iron keel could be jettisoned in sections by disengaging the bolts that held it on, thus causing her to bob corklike to the surface. A glass port in the forward hatch enabled the steersman to see where he was going while submerged, and interior light was supplied by candles, which also served to warn of the danger of asphyxiation by guttering when the oxygen ran low. Practice dives in Mobile Bay had demonstrated that the *Hunley* could stay down about two hours before coming up for air, and she had proved her effectiveness as an offensive weapon by torpedoing and sinking two flatboats there. Her method of attack was quite as novel as her design. Towing at the end of a 200-foot line a copper cylinder packed with ninety pounds of powder and equipped with a percussion fuze, she would dive as she approached her target, pass completely under it, then elevate a bit and drag the towline across the keel of the enemy ship until the torpedo made contact and exploded, well astern of the submarine, whose crew would be cranking hard for a getaway, still underwater, and a return to port for a new torpedo to use on the next victim. Beauregard looked the strange craft over, had her workings explained to him by Hunley, and predicted an end to the Yankee blockade as soon as her newly volunteered crew learned to handle her well enough to launch their one-boat offensive against the U.S. Navy.

Such high hopes were often modified by sudden disappointments, and the *Hunley* was no exception to the general application of the rule. Certain drawbacks were soon as evident here as they had been at Mobile earlier: one being that she was a good deal easier to take down than she was to bring back up, particularly if something went wrong with her machinery, and something often did. She was, in fact — as might have been expected from her combination of primitive means and delicate functions — accident-prone. On August 29, two weeks after her arrival, she was moored to a steamer tied to the Fort Johnson dock, resting her "engine" between dives, when the steamer unexpectedly got underway and pulled her over on her side. Water poured in through the open hatches, front and rear, and she went down so fast that only her skipper and two nimble seamen managed to get out before she hit the bottom. This was a practical demonstration that none of the methods providing for her return to the surface by her own devices would work unless she retained enough air to lift the weight of her iron hull; a started seam or a puncture, inflicted by chance or by enemy action while she was submerged, would mean her end, or at any rate the end of the submariners locked inside her. If this had not been clear before, it certainly was now.

Still, there was no difficulty in finding more volunteers to man her, and Hunley himself, as soon as she had been raised and cleared of muck and corpses, petitioned Beauregard to let him take command. He did so on September 22 and began at once a period of intensive training to familiarize his new crew with her quirks. This lasted just over three weeks. On October 15, after making a series of practice dives in the harbor, she "left the wharf at 9.25 a.m. and disappeared at 9.35. As soon as she sank," the official post-mortem continued, "air bubbles were seen to rise to the surface of the water, and from this fact it is supposed the hole at the top of the boat by which the men entered was not properly closed."

That was the end of Hunley and all aboard, apparently because someone had been careless. It was also thought to be the end of the vessel that bore his name, for she was nine fathoms down. A diver found her a few days later, however, and she was hauled back up again. Beauregard was on hand when her hatch lids were removed. "The spectacle was indescribably ghastly," he later reported with a shudder of remembrance. "The unfortunate men were contorted into all sorts of horrible attitudes, some clutching candles . . . others lying in the bottom tightly grappled together, and the blackened faces of all presented the expression of their despair and agony."

Despite this evidence of the grisly consequences, a third crew promptly volunteered for service under George E. Dixon, an army lieutenant who transferred from an Alabama regiment to the *Hunley* and was also a native of Mobile. Trial runs were renewed in early November, but the method of

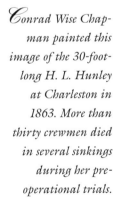

Conrad Wise Chapman painted this image of the 30-foot-long H. L. Hunley at Charleston in 1863. More than thirty crewmen died in several sinkings during her pre-operational trials.

attack was not the same. Horrified by what he had seen when the unlucky boat was raised the second time, Beauregard had ordered that she was never again to function underwater, and she was equipped accordingly with a spar torpedo like the one her rival *David* had used against the *Ironsides,* ten days before she herself went into her last intentional dive. A surface vessel now like all the rest, except that she was still propelled by muscle power, she continued for the next three months to operate out of her base on Sullivan's Island, sometimes by day, sometimes by night. But conditions were never right for an attack; tide and winds conspired against her, and at times the underpowered craft was in danger of being swept out to sea because of the exhaustion of the men along her crankshaft. Finally though, in the early dusk of February 17, with a near-full moon to steer her by, a low-lying fog to screen her, and a strong-running ebb tide to increase her normal four-knot speed, Dixon maneuvered the *Hunley* out of the harbor and set a course for the Federal fleet, which lay at anchor in the wintry darkness, seven miles away.

At 8.45 the acting master of the 1200-ton screw sloop *Housatonic* — more than two hundred feet in length and mounting a total of nine guns, including an 11-inch rifle — saw what he thought at first was "a plank moving [toward us] in the water" about a hundred yards away. By the time he knew better and ordered "the chain slipped, engine backed, and all hands called to quarters" in an attempt to take evasive action and bring his guns to bear, it was too late; "The torpedo struck forward of the mizzen mast, on the starboard side, in line with the magazine." Still trembling from the shock, the big warship heeled to port and went down stern first. Five of her crew were killed or drowned, but fortunately for the others the water was shallow enough for them to save themselves by climbing the rigging, from which they were plucked by rescuers before the stricken vessel went to pieces.

There were no Confederate witnesses, for there were no Confederate survivors; the *Hunley* had made her first and last attack and had gone down with her victim, either because her hull had been cracked by the force of the explosion, only twenty feet away, or else because she was drawn into the vortex of the sinking *Housatonic*. In any case, searchers found what was left of the sloop and the submarine years later, lying side by side on the sandy bottom, just beyond the bar.

★ ★ ★ Quincy Gillmore had been about as unhappy outside Charleston as Beauregard was inside the place, although for different reasons. Six months of siege, of suffering far greater losses than he inflicted, had gained him nothing more than Morris Island, out on the rim of the harbor, and the chance to heave an occasional long-range shell into the city — a practice which his adversary had predicted would win him "a bad eminence in history." That might be, but what bothered Gillmore most was that it seemed to increase rather than lessen the resolution of the defenders. Besides, the next step was up to the navy, and Dahlgren would not take it. The result was stalemate and frustration, a sharp regret on Gillmore's part that he had come down here in the first place. He wanted to be up and doing; he wanted room for maneuver, a chance to fight an enemy he could see; none of which was available to him here. Then in mid-January a letter from the Commander in Chief relieved his claustrophobia by opening vistas to the south. He was to undertake, without delay, the conquest of Florida.

The letter was not sent through regular channels, but was delivered in person by the President's twenty-five-year-old private secretary John Hay, who arrived wearing a brand-new pair of major's leaves on the shoulders of a

Quincy A. Gillmore, who directed the Federal attempt to conquer Florida, had supervised harbor fortification construction, taught engineering, and served as quartermaster at West Point before the war.

brand-new uniform. Moreover, the document he brought with him made it clear that he had been commissioned to play a leading role in the show about to open down the coast. If Gillmore thought it strange at first that the choice for so important a post had been based exclusively on political qualifications — for the young man had had little experience in any other line — he soon perceived, from reading the instructions, that the proposed campaign was intended to be at least as much a political as a military endeavor. "I wish the thing done in the most speedy way possible," Lincoln wrote, "so that, when done, it [will] lie within the range of the late proclamation on the subject."

It was the month-old Proclamation of Amnesty and Reconstruction he meant. He already had agents at work in Louisiana and Arkansas, attempting within the framework of its provisions to establish in them the ten-percent governments he maintained would entitle them to representation in Congress, where their gratitude was expected to prove helpful to the Administration, and it had occurred to him that Florida would make a convenient addition to the list. Hay had Unionist friends there who had written to him, he informed his diary and his chief, "asking me to come down. . . and be their Representative." Lincoln thought it a fine idea. Useful as the young Hoosier was in his present job, he might be even more so in the House. Accordingly, after commissioning him a major and making sure that he was equipped with enough oath-blanks to accommodate the ten percent of Floridians who presumably were weary of rebellion, he gave him the letter of instructions to pass along to Gillmore and wished him success in his venture into an unfamiliar field. "Great good luck and God's blessing go with you, John," he said.

Arriving in South Carolina, Hay assured Gillmore that it was not the President's intention to disrupt his current operations against Charleston, that all he wanted was "an order directing me to go to Florida and open my books of record for the oaths, as preliminary to future proceedings." He soon found, however, that the general was not touchy on that point. Far from considering Lincoln's project an intrusion, Gillmore saw it as an indorsement and extension of a proposal he himself had made in letters to Stanton and Halleck that same week, unaware that Hay was on the way from Washington. "I have in contemplation the occupation of Florida, on the west bank of the Saint Johns River, at a very early day," he announced, requesting their approval. He had it in mind to extend his coastal holdings a hundred miles inland to the Suwannee River, which he explained would enable him: 1) "To procure an outlet for cotton, timber, lumber, turpentine, and other products"; 2) "To cut off one of the enemy's sources of commissary supplies"; 3) "To obtain recruits for my colored regiments"; and 4) — appended after receiving Lincoln's instructions, which amounted to the approval he was seeking — "To inaugurate measures for the speedy restoration of Florida to her allegiance."

In addition to these four "objects and advantages," as he called them, he was also attracted to the venture by the knowledge that the Confederacy had none of its regular troops assigned to the state's defense. The only graybacks there were militia, and Gillmore believed he could walk right over them with a single veteran division from his army lying idle outside Charleston and at Hilton Head, waiting for the navy to take the step it would not take. Now that the President's letter had unleashed him, he was eager to be off, and he fretted because Hay was held up by last-minute administrative details. "There will not be an hour's delay after the major is ready," he informed Lincoln on January 21, and he added: "I have every confidence in the success of the enterprise."

It was another two weeks before the preliminaries had been attended to. Then finally, on February 6, Brigadier General Truman Seymour's division, composed of three brigades of infantry, two regiments of cavalry, and four batteries of artillery — a force of about 8000 in all, mostly Regulars, New Englanders, and Negroes — got aboard twenty transports at Hilton Head and set

★

The navy yard at Hilton Head, South Carolina, served as the staging ground for the Federal invasion of Florida in 1864.

off down the coast, escorted by two gunboats. Next morning the flotilla steamed into the St Johns estuary and docked unopposed at Jacksonville, which had been reduced to little more than ruins by the two previous Federal occupations and deserted by all but about two dozen of its prewar families. Hay went ashore and set up shop, beginning with a line-up at the guardhouse. He explained to the captive rebels that if they took the prescribed oath they would be given certificates of loyalty and allowed to return home; otherwise they would be sent North to prison camps. "There is to be neither force nor persuasion used in this matter," he told them. "You decide for yourselves." Most signed promptly, about half making their marks, and took their leave. Hay turned next to the civilians, and though they were less eager to signify repentance for their transgressions, he succeeded in getting the signatures of a number whom he described as "men of substance and influence," presumably meaning those who still had something left to lose.

Encouraged, he looked forward to lengthening the list as soon as the army extended its occupation and demonstrated that it was here to stay. Mean-

★

time he made a $500 investment in Florida real estate, partly because he knew a hard-times bargain when he saw one, but also by way of establishing residence for the political race that would follow close upon his securing the signatures of ten percent of the qualified electors.

He had reason to believe this would not take long. Gillmore and the navy had been as active in their fields of endeavor as Hay had been in his, and they had also been as successful, if not more so; at least at the outset. Steaming on past Jacksonville after debarking most of the force they had escorted down the coast, the two warships trained their guns on Picolata and Palatka, respectively thirty and fifty miles upstream, and put troops ashore to garrison them, thus establishing firm (and, as it turned out, permanent) control of a coastal region twenty to thirty miles in width and seventy miles in length, east from the St Johns River to the Atlantic and south from Fernandina, near the Georgia line, to below Saint Augustine, which had been reoccupied in late December. What

His main concern was logistics: meaning supplies, primarily food and ammunition, and how to get them forward to the troops as they slogged westward across a sandy waste of stunted oaks, pine trees, and palmettos.

was more, while the navy was consolidating these gains, Gillmore had his troops in motion westward, intent on extending the conquest inland all the way to the Suwannee, as he had said he would do when he first announced his plans.

Florida had two railroads, one running southwest from Fernandina, through Gainesville, to Cedar Key on the Gulf of Mexico, the other due west from Jacksonville to Tallahassee. He took the latter as his route of march, the Atlantic & Gulf Central, his primary objective being Lake City, about sixty miles away. Setting out on February 8, the day after his debarkation, by the following morning he had his cavalry in Baldwin, at the crossing of the two railroads and one third of the way to his goal. His infantry marched in next day, still preceded by the troopers, who pressed on ten miles down the line to Barber's and then another ten to Sanderson, only twenty miles from Lake City. But after advancing half that distance, the cavalry commander, Colonel Guy V. Henry, learned on reaching Olustee that rebel militia were massing in sizable numbers for resistance up ahead; so he turned back. It was well for him and his three small regiments that he did, if he had been counting on infantry support in case of trouble; for when he reëntered Sanderson on the 12th he found that Gillmore was withdrawing to Jacksonville, leaving Seymour to backtrack in his wake and hold Baldwin with the major part of his division while he himself returned to Hilton Head to make further arrangements he had not known were needed, until now.

He too had learned of the rebels massing at Lake City to contest a farther blue advance, and this had served to give him pause. However, his main concern was logistics: meaning supplies, primarily food and ammunition, and how to get them forward to the troops as they slogged westward across a sandy waste of stunted oaks, pine trees, and palmettos. He lacked wagons and mules to draw them, having counted on using the railroad, and though he had plenty of boxcars, captured by Henry's fast-riding troopers before they could be withdrawn beyond the Suwannee, the only locomotive he had on hand was one he had brought with him, which had promptly nullified his foresight by breaking down. So he turned back, better than halfway to his goal, not so much in fear of the gray militia up ahead — although they were reported to be numerous — as in anticipation of what would happen to his soldiers once they had eaten up the six-day rations they carried with them on their march through this barren, inland region. Before returning to Hilton Head to correct in person his miscalculation in logistics, he told Seymour to hold Baldwin at all costs, thus to cover Jacksonville in case the enemy moved against him, but otherwise to be content with consolidating rather than extending his occupation of the coastal region east of the St Johns. That was Gillmore's second miscalculation: not taking sufficiently into account the temperament of his chief subordinate, who would assume command while he himself was up the coast.

A forty-year-old Vermont-born West Pointer, Seymour had seen about as much action as any man on either side in the war, including service as an artillery captain at Sumter when the opening shots were fired. Earlier he had been brevetted twice for bravery in Mexico and the Seminole War, and he had risen about as rapidly as he could have wished in the first two years of the contest still in progress, succeeding to the command of a division in the course of the Seven Days, after which had come Second Bull Run, South Mountain, and Antietam. In all these battles, whether his job was staff or line, he had demonstrated ability; yet somehow, while earning an additional three brevets, he had missed distinction. Then had come a transfer to the Carolina coast, and there too he had performed with credit, especially in the taking of Battery Wagner, where he was severely wounded as a result of his practice of exposing himself under fire. Somehow, though, distinction still eluded him at every turn. And now there was this fruitless westward march across the barrens of North Florida, ended in midcareer by a withdrawal and followed by peremptory instructions for him to remain strictly on the defensive in the absence of a superior whose outstanding characteristic seemed to him to be an unwillingness to assume the risks that went with gain and were in fact the handholds to distinction. Gillmore left

Jacksonville on February 13; Seymour managed to endure four days of inactivity in his nominal, if temporary, position as commander of the Florida expedition. Then on the fifth day he went over to the offensive.

He did this strictly on his own, ostensibly because of a report that the rebels were about to remove the rails from the Atlantic & Gulf Central, which he knew would upset Gillmore's plans for a resumption of the advance to the Suwannee. It was not that he was unaware of the risks involved; he was; the question later was whether he had welcomed or ignored them. For example, garrison detachments had reduced his mobile strength to about 5500 effectives, and though he suspected that the Confederates had more troops than that around Lake City, he knew they were militia to a man and apt therefore to flinch from contact with anything that came at them in a determined manner, which was precisely what he had in mind. Moreover, he intended to make up for the possible disparity in numbers by seizing the initiative and moving with celerity once he had it. "I wish the thing done in the most speedy way possible," Lincoln had said, and Seymour demonstrated his agreement with this approach when he left Jacksonville on February 18 and cleared Baldwin before nightfall.

By sundown of the following day his infantry was beyond Barber's, having covered better than thirty miles of sandy road, and his orders were for the march to be resumed at dawn. For added speed, he advanced in three columns, keeping close on the heels of the cavalry to avoid the delay of having to probe the front or shield the flanks with skirmishers detached from his three infantry brigades. All morning, February 20, he kept his soldiers on the go, slogging through Sanderson and on to Olustee without a rest halt, intent on reaching Lake City before the graybacks had time to get set for the strike. Blown, hungry, and considerably strung out, the three columns converged as they approached Ocean Pond, a swamp just beyond Olustee, around whose southern reaches the road and the railroad passed together along a narrow neck of firm ground with bogs on the left and right. It was here, barely a dozen miles from Lake City and on terrain that was scarcely fit for fighting — at any rate, not the kind of fighting he had in mind — that Seymour first encountered resistance in the form of butternut skirmishers who rose from hiding and took the heads of the three blue columns under fire, then faded back into the palmetto thickets. Recovering as best he could from the surprise, which came all the harder because he had expected to be the inflictor, not the victim, he gave orders for the pursuit to be pressed without delay. It was; but not for long. Within five minutes and two hundred yards, he found himself involved in the battle known thereafter as Olustee or Ocean Pond.

The contest lasted from shortly after noon until about 4 o'clock, not because there was ever much doubt as to the outcome, but simply because that much time was required to make Seymour admit he'd been whipped. In the

Joseph Finegan, commanding the Confederate Department of Middle and Eastern Florida, thwarted the Federal incursion into Florida at Olustee. Later in the year, he fought at Cold Harbor and in the Petersburg siege.

end, it was his own men who convinced him, although the Confederates, with four guns against his sixteen, had been highly persuasive in this regard from the start. Brigadier General Joseph Finegan, a thirty-nine-year-old Irish-born Floridian, had about the same number of troops as his opponent, just over or under 5500, and though they were as green as their commander, an unblooded prewar lumberman and railroader, they were by contrast rested and forewarned, having moved out of Lake City two days ago to dig in along the near end of the swamp-bound neck of land and there await the arrival of the bluecoats on terrain that would cramp their style and limit their artillery advantage. As a result, the butternut militia had only to stand more or less firm and keep shooting, whereas the attackers were obliged to try to maneuver, which was practically impossible, hemmed in as they were on the left and right by spongy ground and blasted from the front by masses of graybacks who also enjoyed the protection of intrenchments.

The fighting consisted mainly of a series of breakdowns and disintegrations which occurred when a number of blue regiments, exposed to such obvious tactical disadvantages, wavered and finally came apart under pressure. A New Hampshire outfit was the first to give way, followed by another of Negro regulars who fled when their colonel was shot down, and total collapse was only forestalled by Seymour's belated permission for the rest to withdraw. They did so in considerable haste and disorder, leaving six of their guns behind them on the field. Early darkness ended the pursuit, which had been delayed by another Negro regiment assigned to rearguard duty. Casualties totaled 1861 for the Federals, including more than 700 killed or captured, while the Confederates lost 946, with fewer than 100 dead or missing. Seymour had at last achieved distinction, but not at all of the kind for which he yearned, since it resulted from the addition of his name to the list of those commanders, North and South, who suffered the soundest thrashings of the war.

Slogging rearward under cover of darkness, the whipped and bleeding survivors were as bitter as they were footsore. "This moment of grief is too sacred for anger," an officer wrote home. But that was by no means the general reaction, which was not unlike the one displayed on the similar withdrawal from the field of Chickamauga, five months ago tonight. If this retreat was on a smaller scale, as far as concerned the number of troops involved, it was at any rate much longer, and it was harder in still other ways. Without nearly enough ambulances or wagons to accommodate the wounded, crude litters had to be improvised, with results that were not only painful for the men being jolted but also exhausting for the bearers. Still, they made good time: better, indeed, than they had made on the speedy outward march. By moonrise they were at Sanderson, ten miles from the scene of their defeat, and they passed through Barber's before daybreak. The second of these two segments was even grimmer than the first, partly because the marchers were wearier, partly too because they lacked by then the disconcerting spur of pursuit, the rebels having halted far in the rear. Now they had time for comprehending what had happened back there at Olustee, and that had perhaps the grimmest effect of all. "Ten miles we wended or crawled along," a participant afterwards said of the small-hours trek from Sanderson to Barber's, "the wounded filling the night air with lamentations, the crippled horses neighing in pain, and the full moon kissing the cold, clammy lips of the dying." Moreover, there was no halt on the 21st at Baldwin, despite previous instructions for holding that vital crossing at all costs, and by sunup of the following morning the head of the column was in Jacksonville, which it had left four days and a hard hundred miles ago.

Gillmore's dismay, on learning of what had happened in his absence and against his orders, was increased by information that the Confederates had advanced beyond Baldwin and were intrenching a line along McGirt's Creek, midway between that place and Jacksonville. Whether this was in preparation for defense or attack he did not know, though it might well be for the latter, since they were reported to have been heavily reinforced from Georgia. In any case, the question was no longer whether he could advance to the Suwannee, as he had formerly intended, but whether he could hold the coastal strip he had seized within a week of his arrival; Beauregard had outfoxed him again, he admitted to his superiors in Washington. "The enemy have thrown so large a force into Florida," he informed Halleck on February 23, "that I judge it to be inexpedient to do more at the present time than hold the line of the Saint Johns River."

One thing he could and did do, however, and that was to relieve Seymour of the command he had abused. But this was plainly a case of locking the stable after the pony was stolen. Certainly it was no help to Hay, who was finding it much harder now to obtain signatures for his oath-blanks. In fact, many who

Slogging rearward under cover of darkness,
the whipped and bleeding survivors were as bitter
as they were footsore.

had signed appeared to regret that they had done so; while others, as he noted in his diary, "refused to sign, on the ground that they were not repentant." It was becoming increasingly clear, with the spread of news of the recent Union defeat, that he and his chief had miscalculated the temper of the people. Florida, the least populous of the Confederate states, had furnished the smallest number of troops for the rebel armies; but that was by no means a fit basis on which to determine her zeal for the secessionist cause, which was indicated far better by the fact that she had given a larger proportion of her eligible men than had any other state. On March 3, within twelve days of the rebel victory at Olustee, Hay frankly confessed: "I am very sure that we cannot now get the President's 10th."

This being so, there was little point in his remaining. Nor did he. After a side excursion to Key West — where he went in hope of picking up a few more signatures, but found instead "a race of thieves and a degeneration of vipers" — he returned somewhat crestfallen to the capital, intending to resume his former duties if his chief would overlook the unhappy events of the past month and take him back.

He found the hostile papers in full bay, charging Lincoln with having "fooled away 2000 men in a sordid attempt to manufacture for himself three additional votes in the approaching Presidential election." Nor did Hay escape their censure as a party to the conspiracy to overawe Florida, not for any true military purpose, but merely to win himself a seat in Congress and deliver a set of committed delegates to the Republican convention. This last, they said, explained the reckless haste that had brought Seymour to defeat; for the convention would be held in June, and the hapless general had been obliged to expose his troops to slaughter in an attempt to carry out his orders to complete the intended conquest of that waste of sand in time for a new government to be formed and delegates to be chosen who would cast their votes for Lincoln's renomination. Returning at the height of the scandal aroused by the failure of his mission, Hay armed himself with extenuating documents for the confrontation with his chief. He expected at least a grilling — for there was enough unpleasant truth in the opposition's charges to make them sting far worse than the usual fabrications — but he was wrong; Lincoln assumed that the young man had done his best in a difficult situation, and did not blame him for the trouble the journalists were making. "There was no special necessity of my presenting my papers," Hay wrote in his diary that night, "as I found he thoroughly understood the state of affairs in Florida and did not seem in the least annoyed by the newspaper falsehoods about the matter."

Others received a different impression of the President's reaction to this latest in the series of attacks designed to expose him as a master of deceit, an unprincipled opportunist, a clod, a tyrant, a bawdy clown, a monster. Earlier that month a White House visitor observed that Lincoln seemed "deeply wounded" by the allegation that he had been willing to pay in blood for votes. As usual, however, even as he was ringed by critics flinging charges at his head, he could see at least one touch of humor in the situation. He told in this connection of a backwoods traveler who got caught one night in a violent storm and who floundered about in the blackness, his sense of direction lost amid blinding zigzags of lightning and deafening peals of thunder, until finally a bolt crashed directly overhead, awesome as the wrath of God, and brought him to his knees, badly frightened. By ordinary not a praying man, he kept his petition brief and to the point. "O Lord," he cried, "if it's all the same to you, give us a little more light and a little less noise!"

★ ★ ★ *W*hile Gillmore and Hay, with Seymour's manic assistance, were failing to bring Florida back into the Union under the terms of the Proclamation of Amnesty and Reconstruction, another quasi-military project which had to do with that document, and which likewise had the President's enthusiastic approval, was moving into its final preparatory stages in Virginia. Aimed at nothing so ambitious as the overnight return of the Old Dominion to its former allegiance, this second venture along those lines was an attempt to see that the people there were acquainted at first hand, rather than through the distorting columns of their local papers or the vituperative speeches of their leaders, with the terms of Lincoln's offer; in which case, it was presumed, a good many of them would be persuaded to see the wisdom of acceptance and the folly of delay. Even if the project fell a long way short of accomplishing the most that could be hoped for, it would at least create doubt and provoke division in the enemy ranks, its authors believed, at a time when the struggle was about to enter its most critical phase. Just as the Florida venture mixed war and politics, so was this Virginia expedition designed to combine a military and a propaganda effort. Lincoln had warned his adversaries that he would not leave "any available card unplayed," and this — though it would go considerably further in bloody intent, before it was over, than he had realized when he approved it — was another example of the fact that he meant exactly what he said.

Designed strictly as a cavalry operation, the project had its beginning in the mind of Judson Kilpatrick, who conceived the notion of launching a bold strike at the Confederate capital, sixty miles in Lee's rear, for the triple purpose of crippling and snarling the lines of supply and communication between the Rapidan and the James, disrupting the rebel government by jangling the nerves of the people who functioned at its center, and freeing the Union captives being held there in increasingly large numbers since the breakdown of the system of exchange. Like his purpose, his motivation was threefold: love of action, desire for acclaim, and envy. Averell having recently been applauded for his successful year-end raid into southwest Virginia, the New Jersey cavalryman planned to win far more applause by striking, not with a lone brigade, but with his whole division, and not at some remote objective on the fringes of the map, as Averell had done, but at the very solar plexus of rebellion. Such a blow would outdo all the horseback exploits that had gone before it, including the highly touted "rides" by Stuart in his heyday. Besides, Kilpatrick did not believe the hit-and-run operation would be nearly as risky, or anyhow as difficult, as it sounded. His information was that Richmond was scantly protected by inexperienced home guardsmen who would not be able to offer serious resistance to an approximately equal number of veteran troopers armed with seven-shot repeaters, not to mention the fact that his strength would be more than doubled, once he broke through the rim of the city's defenses, by the liberation and addition of some 5000 bluecoats reported to be at Libby and on Belle Isle.

A more difficult problem, just now, was how to go about securing the approval he had to have before he could take off southward on the venture he was sure would bring him fame. He had little caution in his makeup, but at any rate he knew better than to propose his scheme to Pleasonton, who might hog it, or to the overcautious Meade, who would be certain to see it as harebrained and reject it in short order. Instead, he took care to communicate in private with certain persons known to be close to the highest authority of all. That was in late January, and the result was about as prompt as he expected. On February 11 a high-priority telegram clicked off the wire from Washington, addressed to the commander of the Army of the Potomac: "Unless there be strong reasons to the contrary, please send Gen. Kilpatrick to us here, for two or three days. A. Lincoln."

"Us" included Stanton, who shared with his chief a staunch, perhaps an extravagant admiration for military boldness, a quality sadly lacking in the upper echelons of the eastern theater, as they saw it, but personified by the bandy-legged general known to the army as "Kill Cavalry." The latter arrived in the capital next morning — the President's fifty-fifth birthday — and was received in private by the Secretary of War. Stanton liked the proposition even better at first hand than he had by hearsay, seeing in it, in addition to the fruits predicted by its author, the possibility of affording a real boost to morale on the home front when the news went out that Federal horsemen had clattered

Described as "a wiry . . . undersized man with black eyes," H. J. Kilpatrick led an ill-fated raid on Richmond.

through the streets of Richmond, striking terror into the hearts of rebel leaders and freeing thousands of blue-clad martyrs from a durance worse than vile. Moreover, having applauded the young brigadier's conception, which was much in line with his own belief as to the manner in which this war should be fought, the Secretary passed along a suggestion from Lincoln that would give the raid an added dimension, and this was that each trooper carry with him a hundred or so copies of the recent amnesty proclamation for distribution along the way.

Kilpatrick pronounced this a splendid notion, then presently, the details having been agreed on, returned to the Rapidan, encouraged and flattered by the confidence thus shown by the head of the War Department — who made it clear that he spoke as well for the Commander in Chief — in a twenty-seven-year-old subordinate, less than three years out of West Point. Hard in his wake, orders came to Culpeper directing that his division be reinforced to a strength of about 4000 for the raid he proposed and that he be given all the assistance he required, including diversionary actions by other units, foot and horse.

Meade was not happy about the project, of which he had known nothing until now. Nor was Pleasonton, who recalled the ill-fated Stoneman raid, which had been similar in purpose and conception, but which had accomplished little except "the loss to the government [of] over 7000 horses, besides the equipments and men left on the road." In short, the chief of cavalry said flatly, the expedition was "not feasible at this time." As for the proposed distribution of the President's proclamation, he suggested that this could be done better, and far cheaper, by undercover agents, and he offered "to have it freely circulated [by this method] in any section of Virginia that may be desired." But nothing came of these objections by the New Jersey cavalryman's immediate superiors. In fact, they were received in Washington as further evidence of the timidity which had crippled the eastern army from the outset. The orders were peremptory, Meade was told; Kilpatrick was to be given a free rein.

About the time of Washington's Birthday, which came ten days after Lincoln's, bales of leaflets reprinting the amnesty proclamation arrived for distribution to the raiders, who were to scatter them broadcast on the way to Richmond. There also arrived from Washington, four days later and only two days short of the jump-off date, a twenty-one-year-old colonel who came highly recommended for his "well-known gallantry, intelligence, and energy" — this last despite a wooden leg and a manner described by an admirer as "soft as a cat's." Ulric Dahlgren was his name. He was the admiral's son, but he preferred the cavalry to the navy because he believed the mounted arm would afford him more and better chances for adventure and individual accomplishment. Commissioned a captain at nineteen by Stanton himself before the war was a year old, he had served in rapid succession on the staffs of Sigel, Burnside, Hooker, and Meade, all of whom had found him useful as well as ornamental, and it had been near Boonsboro, during the pursuit of Lee after Gettysburg, that he received the wound that resulted in the amputation. Once he was able to get about on crutches he went down the coast and convalesced aboard his father's flagship outside Charleston; after which he returned to Washington, where he was jumped three ranks to colonel, reportedly the youngest in the army, and fitted for an artificial leg. While there, he learned of the preparations then in progress for the horseback strike about to be launched against the rebel capital, and he went at once to cavalry headquarters near Brandy to appeal to Pleasonton for permission to go along, despite his crippled condition. Pleasonton sent him to Kilpatrick, who not only acceded to his plea, but also gave him the all-important assignment of leading the way across the Rapidan at the head of a special 500-man detachment, with other hazardous tasks to follow in the course of the ride from that river to the James.

"If successful," he wrote his father, delighted to be back in the war at all, let alone with such a daredevil role to play, "[the raid] will be the grandest thing on record; and if it fails, many of us will 'go up.' I may be captured or I may be 'tumbled over,' but it is an undertaking that if I were not in I should be ashamed to show my face again." He was especially taken with the notion that he would be riding into the very heart of the rebellion, and he added: "If we do not return, there is no better place to 'give up the ghost.' "

Jump-off was set for an hour before midnight, February 28, and proceeded without a hitch, partly because Lee was pulled off balance by Sedgwick, who had shifted his corps upstream that day, as if for a crossing in that direction, while Kilpatrick was massing his 3585 troopers under cover of the woods in rear of Ely's Ford, twenty miles downriver. At the appointed hour they splashed across, mindful of their instructions to "move with the utmost expedition possible on the shortest route past the enemy's right flank." So well did it go that by dawn the column reached Spotsylvania, fifteen miles beyond the Rapidan, unchallenged; at which point, as had been prearranged, Dahlgren and his 500 veered slightly right, while the main body continued to move straight ahead for Richmond, less than fifty miles away. The plan was for the smaller column to cross the James near Goochland, well upstream, so as to approach the rebel capital from the southwest at the same time Kilpatrick came upon it from the north, thereby causing the home-guard defenders to spread thinner and thus expose themselves to the breakthrough that would result in the clatter of Federal hoofs in the streets of their city and the release of 5000 captives from Libby and Belle Isle. Dahlgren's was the longer ride; he would have to avoid delay to arrive on schedule. Kilpatrick saw him off from Spotsylvania, wished him Godspeed as he disappeared into the misty dawn of leap-year day, then continued on his own route, south-southeast, which would bring him and his 3000 to the northern gates of Richmond, if all went as planned, at the same time the young colonel and his detached 500 came knocking at the western gates.

Speed was the watchword; Kilpatrick rode hard and fast, unopposed and apparently unpursued. This last was due in part to a second diversion, back on the Rapidan line. While Sedgwick was feinting westward, George Custer was shifting his 1500-man cavalry brigade even farther in that direction for a dash southward into Albemarle County, a movement designed to attract still more of Lee's attention away from the heavier column rounding his opposite flank. Custer, like Kilpatrick, had certain peculiarities of aspect ("This officer is one of the funniest-looking beings you ever saw," a colonel on Meade's staff wrote home, "and looks like a circus rider gone mad! He wears a huzzar jacket and tight trousers, of faded black velvet trimmed with tarnished gold lace. His head is decked with a little gray felt hat; high boots and gilt spurs complete the costume, which is enhanced by the general's coiffure, consisting in short, dry, flaxen ringlets!") but these gaudy trappings, coupled with a flamboyant personality and a reputation as a glory-hunter, did not interfere with his effectiveness when sheer courage was what was called for — as it was here, off on his own in Lee's left rear, with the task of drawing as many of Stuart's horsemen after him as possible, away from the main effort to the east.

He could scarcely have done a better job, as it turned out. Crossing the river that same Sunday night, some forty miles upstream from Ely's Ford, he threatened Charlottesville next day and returned to the north bank of the Rapidan on Tuesday, March 1, having ridden more than a hundred miles through hostile territory, burned three large grist mills filled with flour and grain, and captured about fifty graybacks and 500 horses, all without the loss of a man and only a few wounded. So well indeed had he carried out his mission, particularly with regard to attracting the rebel cavalry's attention, that he was notified on his return, officially and in writing, of Pleasonton's "entire satisfaction . . . and gratification . . . at the prompt manner in which the duties assigned to you have been performed."

General George A. Custer (with braided sleeve) questions rebel prisoners during a diversionary raid in February 1864.

★

Before Custer returned to the Union lines Kilpatrick was knocking at the gates of Richmond. Across the North Anna by noon of February 29, he had paused astride the Virginia Central at Beaver Dam Station, midway to his objective, and after setting fire to the depot and other installations, thus to discourage any pursuit by rail once Lee found out that some 4000 blue raiders were menacing the capital in his rear, pressed on to make camp near the South Anna by nightfall. An hour past midnight he roused his sleeping troopers and was off again through the darkness, undeterred by an icy rainstorm or the fact that he had received no answering signal when he sent up rockets to indicate his position to Dahlgren, whose detachment was somewhere off to the west. "No rockets could be seen for any distance on such a night as that," an officer was to note, recalling that the "sharp wind and sleet forced men to close their eyes" as they rode southward, their wet clothes frozen stiff as armor. By daylight they were over the Chickahominy near Ashland, and at 10 o'clock in the morning, having covered sixty miles of road in the past thirty-five hours, they came jogging down the Brook Pike to within sight of Richmond and range of its outer fortifications, five miles from the heart of town.

No sooner did they appear than they were taken under fire. Kilpatrick brought up his six guns for counterbattery work and prepared to overrun the defenders, "believing that if they were citizen soldiers" — by which he meant home guardsmen — "I could enter the city." So he reported some weeks later, in the calmness of his tent. One thing that bothered him now, though, was that the boom and clatter of his engagement had drawn no reply from Dahlgren, who should have arrived simultaneously on the far side of the James, there to create the prearranged diversion, but who had either been delayed or gobbled up. Another matter for concern was that the rebels up ahead were doing a highly professional job of defending their position. They were in fact part-time volunteers — government clerks, old men, and boys, considerably fewer in number than the bluecoats to their front, and serving antiquated or worn-out guns long since replaced by new ones in Lee's army — but they handled their pieces with such precision that Kilpatrick began to believe that they had been reinforced by regulars. "They have too many of those damned guns!" he fumed, riding his line amid shell-bursts and withholding the order to charge until he could better determine what stood between him and the breakthrough he intended; "they keep opening new ones on us all the time."

It was strange, this sudden transformation in a hell-for-leather commander who up to now had fairly ached to put his troopers inside Richmond. He had worked all the angles to circumvent his immediate superiors, whose timidity he had seen as the main obstacle to an undertaking that simply could not fail once it got past their disapproval, and had ridden a hard sixty miles through hostile country, bristling with aggressiveness and chafing with impa-

★

tience all the way. Yet now that he had come within plain view of his goal — the goal, for that matter, of every blue-clad soldier in the eastern theater — he declined to risk the last brief sprint, half a mile down the turnpike, then past or through or over "those damned guns," which were all that stood between him and the completion of the mission he had designed with his own particular talents in mind, or anyhow his notion of those talents. It was unquestionably strange, but perhaps it was not as sudden as it seemed; perhaps it had been this way all along, behind the swagger and the blustering impatience.

In any case he limited his aggressiveness, here on the outskirts of his objective, to a tentative sparring match, keeping one ear cocked for some indication that Dahlgren and his daredevil 500 were knocking at the gates beyond the James. After six or seven hours of this, the rebel guns had indeed grown in numbers, along with their infantry support, as reinforcements were hustled to the threatened sector from others undisturbed along the defensive rim, and Kilpatrick finally arrived at a decision. "Feeling confident that Dahlgren had failed to cross

At 10 o'clock, unable to sleep or rest — in part because of the wet and the cold, in part because of his fret at having failed — Kilpatrick remounted his troopers and prepared to launch a night attack down the Mechanicsville road . . .

the river, and that an attempt to enter the city at that point would but end in a bloody failure," he later reported, "I reluctantly withdrew." He fell back northeastward, recrossing the Chickahominy at Meadow Bridge to give his men and horses some badly needed sleep in the sodden fields around Mechanicsville, where Lee had opened his Seven Days offensive, just over twenty months ago.

There had been no fighting here since then, but presently there was. At 10 o'clock, unable to sleep or rest — in part because of the wet and the cold, in part because of his fret at having failed — Kilpatrick remounted his troopers and prepared to launch a night attack down the Mechanicsville road, avoiding the stoutly held pike to the west, in order to achieve a penetration that would last no longer than it took to free the prisoners and come back out again. Before he could get his weary men in line, however, he was himself attacked by rebel horsemen who came at him from the direction of Yellow Tavern, out of the darkness in his rear. Though he managed to beat off this assault, all thoughts of resuming the offensive gave way at once to the problem of survival: especially when he learned, as he soon did, that the attackers were not "citizen soldiers," which were all he had faced till now, but regulars from Wade Hampton's division, who had taken up the belated pursuit from the Rapidan line and then had narrowed the gap between him and them while he was sparring with Richmond's defenders this afternoon. His concern was no longer with the liberation of the prisoners in the city; it was rather how to keep from joining them as a prisoner himself.

Once more his decision was to withdraw northeastward, and this he did, effecting a skillful disengagement to make camp at dawn near Bethesda Church, midway between the Chickahominy and the Pamunkey. Here he remained all morning, March 2, fighting off regular and irregular Confederates who were gathering in ever larger numbers all around him in the woods and swamps. He kept hoping to hear from Dahlgren, but he did not. At noon he abandoned his vigil, together with all hope of entering Richmond, and withdrew to make camp at Tunstall's Station, near McClellan's old base at White House. There at last he was joined that night by a captain and 260 men from Dahlgren's detachment. They had a gloomy tale to tell, though they did not know the even gloomier ending, which was occurring at about that same time, some dozen air-line miles to the northeast.

Despite the almost constant rain, which made for heavy going, Dahlgren had set a rapid pace after he and his picked 500 turned off from the main body at Spotsylvania before sunup, leap-year morning. Proceeding south through Fredericks Hall, where he called a midday halt to feed the horses, he crossed the South Anna late that night and rode into Goochland, thirty miles up the James from the rebel capital, as March 1 was dawning. Here he picked up a young Negro named Martin Robinson, a slave from a nearby plantation, who offered to show him a place where the bridgeless river could be forded. The colonel was in excellent spirits, for he had kept to a difficult schedule and was about to get his troopers into position for the final dash that would put them in southside Richmond before noon, just as he had promised Kilpatrick he would do.

So he thought; but not for long. Arriving at the intended crossing — Jude's Ford, it was called — he found the river on the boom, swollen by the two-day rain and running too swift to be breasted; whereupon the handsome young colonel, whose manner was said to be "soft as a cat's," showed his claws. Although the guide appeared to be quite as surprised as he himself was at the condition of the ford, Dahlgren suspected treachery, and in his anger at having been thwarted — for it was clear now, if nothing else was, that he could not reach his objective either on time or from the appointed direction — ordered him hanged. This was accomplished with dispatch there by the river, one end of a picket rope being flung across a convenient limb while the other was fastened snugly about the neck of the Negro, whose protests were cut short when he left the ground. Without further delay, and almost before the suspended man had ended his comic-dreadful jig, the blue column was back in motion, trotting east-ward down the north bank of the James, its commander watching intently for some sign of a ford shallow enough to be used.

Finding none he paused occasionally to set fire to a grist mill or damage a lock in the left-bank canal, which delayed him still more. It was late afternoon by the time he cleared Short Pump, eight miles from Richmond, and heard the boom of guns in the misty northeast distance. He quickened the pace, but presently he too encountered resistance, with the result that by the time he got close to the city Kilpatrick had withdrawn. So far as Dahlgren could tell, alone in the gathering dusk with rebel militia all around him, his horses sagging with fatigue and a hard rain coming down, the main body had simply vanished. His instructions in such a case — that is, once the raid was over: as it now definitely was, though not at all in the manner Kilpatrick had predicted — called for a return to the Union lines, either by way of Fredericks-burg or down the York-James peninsula.

He chose the former route, turning off to the north, away from Richmond and across the Chickahominy, well above Meadow Bridge. His troopers had had little sleep in the past three nights, and by now the column had split in two, some 300 of the men becoming separated from the rest in the gloom and confusion. These were the ones — 260 of them, at any rate; about forty were captured or shot from their saddles next day — who joined the main body at Tunstall's the following night. Meanwhile, Dahlgren and the remaining 200 managed to cross the Pamunkey, a few miles north of there, and continued on through the darkness to the Mattaponi, exchanging shots with roving bands of rebels all the way. This stream too they crossed, but they got only a bit far-ther. Approaching King and Queen Courthouse, just beyond the river, they stumbled into an ambush laid in their path by Fitz Lee's regulars, who had also arrived from the Rapidan by now. Dahlgren, riding point, decided to brazen or bluff his way through; or perhaps he recalled that he had told his father there was no better place to die. "Surrender, you damned rebels," he cried, flourishing his revolver, "or I'll shoot you!" The answering volley unhorsed him with four bullets in his body, and witnesses afterwards testified that before he struck the ground he had already given up what he had called the ghost.

Most of those with him were likewise killed or captured, a number being flushed from hiding next morning by pursuers who put bloodhounds on their trail. Kilpatrick was incensed when he heard of this unchivalrous practice from a dozen of Dahlgren's men who managed to get through to him a few days later at Yorktown, where he ended his withdrawal down the Peninsula, safe within the Union lines. He spoke, in his official report, of the colonel's death as "murder" — a curious charge for a professional to make — but he did not hesi-tate, in that same document, to blame the dead man for the unhappy outcome

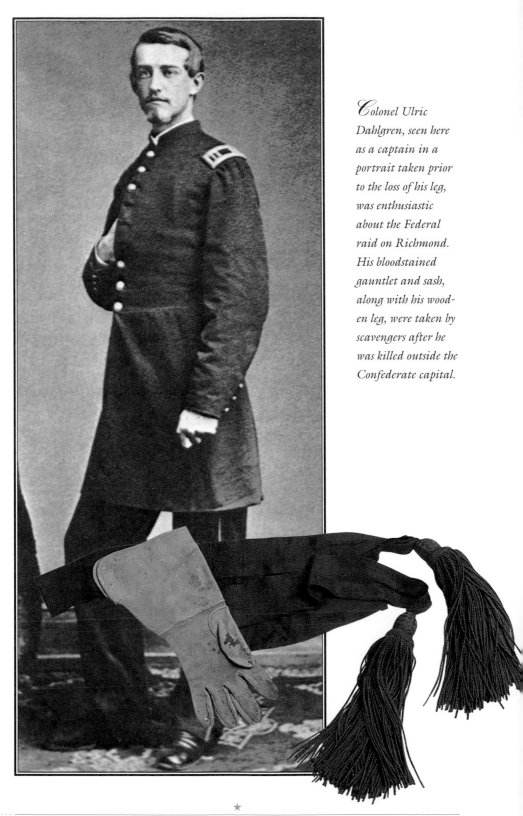

Colonel Ulric Dahlgren, seen here as a captain in a portrait taken prior to the loss of his leg, was enthusiastic about the Federal raid on Richmond. His bloodstained gauntlet and sash, along with his wooden leg, were taken by scavengers after he was killed outside the Confederate capital.

of the project he himself had planned and led. "I am satisfied that if Colonel Dahlgren had not failed in crossing the river," he declared, ". . . I should have entered the rebel capital and released our prisoners." As it was, instead of decreasing the prison population of Richmond, he had increased it by some 300 veteran troopers (his total loss was 340, but a good many of them were killed) and in addition had lost 583 horses in the course of the ride, plus another 480 too broken down to be of any further use when it was over. About the only profit he could point to was the incidental damage inflicted on various installations along the way, together with the claim that "several thousand of the President's amnesty proclamations were scattered throughout the entire country."

In point of fact, a sizable proportion of these last had been unloaded as dead weight, heaved overboard into roadside ditches when the project degenerated into a race for survival, and whatever of propaganda value was derived from the scattering of Lincoln's amnesty offer had been considerably offset by the hard-handed excesses of the blue troopers engaged in an expedition whose most lamented casualty, according to a Richmond editor, was "a boy named Martin, the property of Mr David Meems, of Goochland." Even so, the resentments stirred up in the course of the raid were mild indeed, compared to those that developed on both sides when it was over: particularly in regard to Ulric Dahlgren, whose zeal was even more in evidence after his death than it had been before he toppled from his horse near King and Queen. His body was subjected to various indignities, including the theft of his artificial leg, the clumsy removal of one of his fingers to get at a ring he was wearing, and the scavenging of other of his private possessions, such as his watch, his boots, and even his clothes.

News of these atrocities created a stir of outrage in the North, but this in turn was overmatched by the furor that followed in the South upon the publication of certain papers found among his personal effects. These included the draft of an address to his command and a detailed set of instructions for what he called "a desperate undertaking." "We will cross the James River into Richmond," he had written, "destroying the bridges after us and exhorting the released prisoners to destroy and burn the hateful city; and do not allow the rebel leader Davis and his traitorous crew to escape." Thus the proposed address, though there was no evidence that it had been delivered. The instructions were more specific. "The men must keep together and well in hand," he urged, "and once in the city it must be destroyed and Jeff Davis and cabinet killed. Pioneers will go along with combustible material."

To Southerners, when these exhortations to arson and assassination were released in print, it appeared that this amounted to hoisting the black flag, and they called bitterly for emulation of the example set — conveniently forgetting, it would seem, Quantrill's previous excesses out in Kansas. One of the angriest among them was Seddon, who sent copies of the documents to Lee,

*These papers, found on Ulric Dahlgren's
body, sparked furious outrage in the South
and fierce denials in the North.*

stating that in his opinion their "diabolical character" required "something more
than a mere informal publication in our newspapers. My own inclinations are toward the execution of at least a portion of those captured at the time. . . . I desire
to have the benefit of your views and any suggestions you may make." Lee
replied that he too was shocked by the details of this "barbarous and inhuman
plot," but that execution of the captured troopers would bring retaliation, and he
wanted no part of a hanging-match with the Yankees. Besides, he told the Secretary, "I do not think that reason and reflection would justify such a course.
I think it better to do right, even if we suffer in so doing, than to incur the re-
proach of our consciences and posterity." Instead he sent the inflammatory docu-

ments across the lines to Meade, together with a note inquiring "whether the designs and instructions of Colonel Dahlgren, as set forth in these papers . . . were authorized by the United States Government or by his superior officers, and also whether they have the sanction and approval of those authorities."

Meade investigated the matter and replied "that neither the United States Government, myself, nor General Kilpatrick authorized, sanctioned, or approved the burning of the city of Richmond and the killing of Mr Davis and cabinet, nor any other act not required by military necessity and in accordance with the usages of war." He also included, for whatever it was worth, a letter from Kilpatrick, impugning the authenticity of the papers. "But I regret to say," Meade privately informed his wife, "Kilpatrick's reputation, and collateral evidence in my possession, rather go against this theory."

There the matter rested, so far at least as Meade and Lee were concerned. As for Lincoln, he too was willing to let it lie, if it only would, and he did not call, as he had done after the frustration of the first of his two attempts to extend the influence of his amnesty proclamation, for "more light"; there had been quite enough of that by now. Both failures were depressing for him to look back on, especially the second. The Florida expedition had been merely a fiasco, a military embarrassment, but the Kilpatrick raid was that and more, adding as it did a deeper bitterness to a fratricidal struggle which, in all conscience, was bitter enough already. It was as if Lincoln, in attempting to soothe and heal the national wounds, had reached blindly into the medicine chest and mistaken an irritant for a salve. That this had been the effect was shown in part by the reaction of newspapers North and South. Calling hotly for reprisal, the Richmond *Examiner* now saw the conflict as "a war of extermination, of indiscriminate slaughter and plunder," while the *New York Times* exulted in the damage done by the raiders in Virginia and gloated over reports brought back of "the large number of dilapidated and deserted dwellings, the ruined churches with windows out and doors ajar, the abandoned fields and workshops, the neglected plantations." As for the slave Martin Robinson, whose body had been left dangling beside unusable Jude's Ford, he had met "a fate he so richly deserved," according to the *Times,* because he had "dared to trifle with the welfare of his country."

That was what they had come to, South and North, as the war moved toward and into its fourth and bloodiest spring.

★　★　★

★

Harper's Weekly correctly portrayed the bitter cold of Grant's 1864 inspection tour as he (front right) crosses the mountains between Knoxville and Barbourville.

THREE

Sherman, Meridian; Forrest

1864 ★ ★ ★ ★ ★ For Grant, the three-month span of comparative idleness that came after the storming of Missionary Ridge was nothing like the one that had followed his earlier triumph at Vicksburg. His manner then had been that of a man not only uncertain of the future, but also doubtful about the present, with time on his hands and no notion of how to use it. Lacking in effect an occupation, what he mainly had been, through that diffi-cult time — after as well as before the New Orleans horseback accident, which had added pain without distraction and immobility without relaxation — was bored. That was by no means the case now. For one thing, there was his vast new department to be inspected, most of which he had had no chance to visit, even briefly, until the Chattanooga siege was lifted.

After a well-earned Christmas rest, he went in early January to Knoxville, then up through Cumberland Gap to Barbourville, from there by way of Lexington to Louisville, and finally back down through Nashville to his start-ing point, with the added satisfaction of having solved a number of supply and security problems all along the route. He had always enjoyed travel, especially when it took him to new places, and what was more the trip presented many of the aspects of a triumphal tour. "All we needed was a leader," a wounded private had told him when he climbed Missionary Ridge in the wake of the men who

★

had carried it, and that was the reaction wherever he went on his swing through East Tennessee and Central Kentucky. *"Hail to the Chief,* both words and air, greeted him at every stopping place," an associate was to recall.

Nor was this enthusiasm by any means limited to those in uniform. Called to St Louis immediately afterwards by the supposedly dangerous illness of one of his children (a false alarm, as it turned out, for the crisis was past when he arrived) he had no sooner checked into the Lindell Hotel — "U. S. Grant, Chattanooga," he signed the register — than he was besieged by admirers with invitations, including one to a banquet tendered in his honor by two hundred leading citizens, determined to outdo in lavishness the affair put on five months ago by their commercial rivals down in Memphis. This he accepted, along with a resolution of thanks from the Common Council. If he was modest in his demeanor at such functions, and brief in his response to speeches of praise, that did not mean that he enjoyed them any less. The fact was, he enjoyed them very much, comparing the treatment accorded him now with the attitude he had encountered in prewar days, a brief five years ago, when he tried his hand at selling real estate in this same city and hardscrabble farming just outside it, and failed at both so thoroughly that he had been reduced to peddling firewood in its streets. This he knew was the way of the world, but he enjoyed the drama of the contrast between then and now, especially here in his wife's home state, where the opinion once had been fairly unanimous, not only that she had married beneath her station, but also that she had saddled herself with a husband who turned out to be a failure in his chosen line of work and a ne'er-do-well in several others.

In addition to these honors done him at first hand, others came from a distance, including three that arrived in rapid order from the seat of government before the year was out. When, amid salutes and illuminations celebrating the Chattanooga triumph, news spread throughout the North that Knoxville too had been delivered, the President coupled his announcement of the victory with a recommendation that the people gather informally in their churches to pay homage to the Almighty "for this great advancement of the national cause," and he followed this next day, December 8, with a personal message to Grant, who passed it along in a general order: "Understanding that your lodgment at Chattanooga and Knoxville is now secure, I wish to tender you, and all under your command, my more than thanks — my profoundest gratitude — for the skill, courage, and perseverance with which you and they, over so great difficulties, have effected that important object. God bless you all." Congress, not to be outdone, passed before Christmas a joint resolution thanking the Illinois general and his men "for their gallantry and good conduct in the battles in which they have been engaged" and providing for "a gold medal to be struck, with suitable emblems, devices, and inscriptions, to be presented to Major General Grant . . . in the name of the people of the United States of America." In

★

time the medal was forwarded as directed, bearing on one side a profile of the general, surrounded by a laurel wreath and a galaxy of stars, and on the other a figure of Fame holding a trumpet and a scroll inscribed with the names of his victories. The motto was "Proclaim liberty throughout the Land."

Meantime a bill was offered to revive the grade of lieutenant general — previously held only by George Washington and Winfield Scott, the former briefly, the latter merely by brevet — for the purpose of assuring that Grant, for whom alone it was intended, would assume by virtue of that lofty rank the post now occupied by Halleck, who stood above him on the list of major generals. Senator James Doolittle of Wisconsin, for one, was specific in his reasons for supporting the proposal. So far in the war, he declared with an enthusiasm that avoided understatement, Grant had won 17 battles, captured 100,000 prisoners, and taken 500 pieces of artillery; "He has organized victory from the beginning, and I want him in a position where he can organize *final* victory and bring it to our armies and put an end to this rebellion."

Doolittle's colleagues wanted final victory, too, and agreed that the probable way to get it would be to apply the western formula in the East; but a majority shared two objections to the course proposed. One was that Grant was needed in the field, not behind a desk in the capital — even if the desk was that of the general-in-chief — and the other was an ingrained fear of creating a military Grand Lama who might someday develop political ambitions and use the army to further them. As a result, the bill failed to pass.

On the face of it, this seemed no great loss, since Grant by then had already offered the government his solution to the problem of how to win the war, only to have it rejected out of hand. Reverting to the proposal he had made soon after the fall of Vicksburg, he sent Charles Dana to Washington in mid-December to lay before his superiors a plan for holding the line of the Tennessee with a skeleton force while the rest of his troops steamed down the Mississippi to New Orleans, from which point they would move against Mobile and reduce it, then march through Alabama and across Georgia, living off the abundance of the Confederate heartland as they went. Meantime the Virginia army would pin Lee down by taking the offensive, and in this connection he suggested that Meade be replaced by Sherman or Baldy Smith, who could better appreciate the need for coördinating the eastern and the western efforts.

Presently Dana wired Grant that he had explained the scheme to Lincoln, Stanton, and Halleck, all three of whom had seen considerable merit in it: aside, that is, from the risk to which it would expose the weakened Union center while the bulk of the troops from there were on the way downriver. That drawback made it sound to them like something devised by McClellan; which plainly would not do. Besides, they wanted no more Chickamaugas, especially none that would be followed up by the victors, who presumably would do just

★

that if they were given the second chance this seemed to offer. In short —
except for that part of it favoring Meade's replacement by Smith, which all three
chiefs applauded as an excellent idea, despite some misgivings about Baldy's
"disposition and personal character" — Grant's proposal was turned down.
Dana added, though, that the trio had welcomed his suggestions and had said
that they would like to hear more of them, if he had any more of them in mind.

He did indeed. Still with his eye on Mobile, he then proposed a dual
offensive against that place and Atlanta, the two drives to be launched simultaneously from New Orleans and Chattanooga, while the eastern army gave up its
weary attempt to capture Richmond from the north and landed instead on the
North Carolina coast in order to approach the rebel capital from the south,
astride its lines of supply and communication. He said nothing more about replacing Meade with Sherman — probably because he had decided he would
need him to lead one of the two western columns — or with Smith, who by
now had begun to exercise the talent for contention that had kept him in hot
water most of his military life and would in time cause Grant, who once had
seemed to think he hung the moon, to refer to him as "a clog." In his reply,
which incorporated Lincoln's and Stanton's views as well as his own, Halleck did
not mention Baldy either, no doubt assuming that Grant had confirmed their
misgivings about the Vermonter's "disposition," but limited himself to an assessment of the strategy involved in the proposal for a double-pronged offensive, East and West. It would not do. Not only did it commit the cardinal sin of
attempting two big things at once in each of the two theaters; it also required
more troops than were available in either. If attempted, it would expose both
Washington and Chattanooga to risks the government simply could not run,
and moreover it showed the flawed conception of a commander who made enemy cities his primary objective, rather than enemy armies, as the President had
lately been insisting must be done if this war was ever to be won. In Halleck's
opinion, Grant would do better to concentrate on the problems at hand in Tennessee and North Georgia, and leave the large-scale thinking to those who were
equipped for it. Just as Meade's objective was Lee's army, Grant's was Johnston's, and both were to keep it firmly in mind that neither Washington nor
Chattanooga — nor, for that matter, East Tennessee, the region of Lincoln's
acutest concern — was to be exposed to even the slightest danger while they
attempted to carry out their separate missions of destroying the rebel masses
in the field before them.

Sherman had returned by now from Knoxville. Grant informed him
that the spring campaign, which would open as soon as the roads were fit for
marching, would be southward against Joe Johnston and Atlanta, and every
available man in both his and Thomas's armies would be needed for what
promised to be the hardest fighting of the war. The redhead was all for it; but

★

*William T. Sherman ponders his next
move during the Meridian campaign in this
idealized portrait from Harper's Weekly.*

first he wanted to put an end to disruptions that had developed in the department he had left to come to Tennessee. In his absence, guerillas had taken to firing at steamboats from the banks of the big river, north and south of Vicksburg, and he did not intend to abide this outrage. "To secure the safety of the navigation of the Mississippi River," he declared, "I would slay millions. On that point

I am not only insane, but mad. . . . I think I see one or two quick blows that will astonish the natives of the South and will convince them that, though to stand behind a big cottonwood and shoot at a passing boat is good sport and safe, it may still reach and kill their friends and families hundreds of miles off. For every bullet shot at a steamboat, I would shoot a thousand 30-pounder Parrotts into even helpless towns on Red, Ouachita, Yazoo, or wherever a boat can float or soldier march." To those who objected to this as war against civilians, he made the point that if rebel snipers could "fire on boats with women and children in them, we can fire and burn towns with women and children."

Angry, he grew angrier by the week. Taking dinner at the home of a Union-loyal Nashville matron, for example, he turned on his hostess when she began to upbraid him for the looting his troops had done on the march to Knoxville. "Madam," he replied, "my soldiers have to subsist themselves even if the whole country must be ruined to maintain them. There are two armies here. One is in rebellion against the Union; the other is fighting for the Union. If either must starve to death, I propose it shall not be the army that is loyal." This said, he added in measured tones: "War is cruelty. There is no use trying to reform it. The crueler it is, the sooner it will be over."

His main fear just now was that the guerillas along the Lower Mississippi, emboldened by the example of the snipers, would band together in sufficient strength to attack the reduced garrisons at various river ports and thus undo much that had been accomplished, at a considerable expense of Federal blood and ingenuity, in the past year. It was Sherman's notion — a notion made more urgent by the need for reducing those garrisons still further in order to furnish additional troops for the campaign scheduled to open in North Georgia in late March or early April — to return to Mississippi between now and then, rather than keep his veteran soldiers lying idle in their winter camps, and nip this threat of renewed obstruction in the bud. As he put it in mid-December, after discussing the problem with Grant, "I think in all January and part of February I can do something in this line." He did not propose to waste his energies in running down individual snipers, which would be like trying to rid a swamp of mosquitoes by swatting them one by one, but rather to destroy the economy — the society, even, if need be — that afforded them subsistence. The way to do this, he maintained, was to wreck their production and transportation facilities so thoroughly that they would have nothing left to defend and nothing left to live on if they attempted resistance for its own sake.

What was more, the situation there seemed made to order for the execution of such a project. Less than two hundred miles east of Jackson was Selma, Alabama, whose cannon foundry and other manufacturing installations Jefferson Davis had admired on his October visit, and roughly midway between them was Meridian, where three vital railroads intersected and which served as a storage and distribution center, not only for industrial products from the east, but also for grain and cattle from the fertile Black Prairie region just to the north. A rapid march by a sizable force, eastward from Vicksburg, then back again for a total distance of about five hundred miles, could be made within the two available months, he believed, and the smashing of these two major objectives, together with the widespread destruction he intended to accomplish en route, would assure a minimum of trouble for the skeleton command he would leave behind when he came back upriver to rejoin Grant for the drive on Atlanta — which Johnston, incidentally, would be much harder put to defend without the rations and guns now being sent to him from Meridian and Selma. That was what the Ohioan had had in mind when he spoke of "one or two blows that will astonish the natives."

There were, as he saw it, three main problems, each represented by an enemy commander who would have to be dealt with in launching this massive raid, first across the width of Mississippi and then beyond the Tombigbee to a

"Madam, my soldiers have to subsist themselves even if the whole country must be ruined to maintain them."

— William T. Sherman

point nearly halfway across Alabama. One was Polk, who had in his camps of instruction at Demopolis, between Meridian and Selma, the equivalent of two divisions with which to oppose him. Another was Johnston, who might send heavy detachments rearward by rail to catch him far from base and swamp him. The third was Forrest, who by now had attracted a considerable number of recruits to the cavalry division he was forming in North Mississippi and could be expected to investigate, in his usual slashing manner, any blue activity within reach. Discussing these problems with Grant, Sherman arrived at answers to all three.

As for the first, he would employ no less than four divisions in his invasion column — two from McPherson's corps at Vicksburg and two from Hurlbut's at Memphis, which he would pick up on his way downriver — for a total of 20,000 infantry, plus about 5000 attached cavalry and artillery. That should take care of Polk, who could muster no better than half that many: unless, that is, he was reinforced by Johnston, and Grant agreed to discourage this by having Thomas menace Dalton. Forrest, the remaining concern, was to be attended to by a special force under W. Sooy Smith, recently placed at the head of all the cavalry in the Army of the Tennessee. At the same time the main body started east from Vicksburg, Smith was to set out south from West Tennessee, with instructions to occupy and defeat Forrest on the way to a link-up with Sherman at Meridian, from which point he and his troopers would take the lead on the march to Selma. His superiors saw, of course, that his more or less incidental defeat of Forrest, en route to the initial objective, was a lot to ask; but to make certain that he did not fail they arranged for him to be reinforced to a strength of 7000, roughly twice the number Forrest had in his green command. In any case, having arrived at this solution to the third of the three problems, Grant and his red-haired lieutenant parted company for a time, the latter to enjoy a Christmas leave with his family in Ohio while the former set out, shortly afterward, on the triumphal inspection tour through East Tennessee and Kentucky, followed by what turned out to be a pleasant visit to St Louis, where he was dined and toasted by civic leaders who once had looked askance at him as a poor catch for a Missouri girl.

In Memphis by mid-January, Sherman found Hurlbut busy carrying out instructions he had sent him to prepare two divisions for the trip downriver and the long march that would follow. While there, he also conferred with Smith, stressing the need for promptness and a vigorous celerity if his horsemen, with nearly twice the distance to cover from their starting point at nearby Collierville, were to reach Meridian at the same time as the foot soldiers, who would set out simultaneously from Vicksburg. Something else he stressed as well, which if neglected could bring on a far direr result than being thrown off schedule. This was what he referred to as "the nature of Forrest as a man, and of his peculiar force," a factor he first had learned to take into account at Fallen Timbers, after Shiloh, where his attempt at a pursuit had been brought to a sudden and unceremonious halt by one of the Tennessean's headlong charges, delivered in defiance not only of the odds, but also of the tactics manuals he had never read. "I explained to him," Sherman said afterwards of this conference with his chief of cavalry, "that in his route he was sure to encounter Forrest, who always attacked with a vehemence for which he must be prepared, and that, after he had repelled the first attack, he must in turn assume the most determined offensive, overwhelm him and utterly destroy his whole force." Without scoffing at the danger, Smith exhibited a confidence in the numerical advantage his superior's foresight had assured him for the impending confrontation with the so-called Wizard of the Saddle.

Meantime Hurlbut completed his preparations. On the 25th he embarked with his two divisions, and Sherman followed two days later. By February 1 — the date set for Smith to begin his nearly 250-mile ride from Collierville, southeast to Okolona, then down the Mobile & Ohio to Meridian, wrecking and burning as he went — all the appointed elements of the infantry column were on hand at Vicksburg.

Sherman spent another two days making certain that all was in order

Federal general Stephen A. Hurlbut was a veteran of the Seminole War and a congressman from Illinois when the war broke out. He commanded the XVI Corps in the Meridian campaign.

for the march, which necessarily would be made without a base of supplies, and assessing the latest intelligence from spies beyond the lines. Polk by now had shifted his headquarters westward across the Tombigbee, from Demopolis to Meridian, and had posted his two divisions at Canton and Brandon, respectively under Loring and Sam French, twenty miles north and twelve miles east of Jackson, while his cavalry, under Stephen Lee, patrolled the region between the Pearl and the Big Black. Far from being alarmed by this, the northern commander was pleased to find his adversaries nearer than he had supposed; for they numbered barely half his strength, with 28 guns opposing 67 in the blue column, and the sooner he came to grips with them, the sooner they would be disposed of as a possible deterrent to his eastward progress and the destruction of everything of value in his path. Intending to move light, without tents or baggage even for corps commanders or himself, he had prescribed a minimum of equipment — "The expedition is one of celerity," he said, "and all things must tend to that" — but, even so, the twenty-day supply of such essentials as hardtack, salt, and coffee, together with ammunition and medical stores, required a 1000-wagon train.

On February 3, having assured himself that all was as he had required, he passed the order that put his four divisions in motion for the Big Black River, one third of the way to Jackson, which in turn was a third of the way to Meridian, where Smith was to join him for the march on Selma, another hundred miles along the railroad he would follow all the way.

★ ★ ★   The march was in two columns, a corps in each, and so rapid that by nightfall both were over the river, trains and all, covering mile after eastward mile of ground for which they had fought in May, while headed in the opposite direction. Now as then, the weather was bright, the roads firm, and the soldiers in high spirits. They reached Edwards next day, swung past Champion Hill to end the third day's march at Bolton, and camped near Clinton the fourth night, within a dozen miles of the Mississippi capital. So far, the only resistance they had encountered was from small bands of cavalry; Lee was trying to slow their advance, and thus gain time for the two Confederate divisions to concentrate beyond the Pearl and there dispute a crossing. But Sherman saw through the design. Refusing to be delayed, he brushed the horsemen aside with his guns and kept his veterans slogging with such speed that Lee had no opportunity to destroy the pontoons of a large bridge, thrown across the river just beyond Jackson, before the Federals marched in on February 7. Twice already, in the past nine months, the torch had been put to this unfortunate town; now Sherman re-re-burned it, meantime pressing on for an uncontested crossing of the Pearl.

Loring and French were in retreat by then, on opposite sides of the river — the former scuttling northward and the latter to the east, back to the places they had advanced from — having failed to get together in time to challenge the invaders at the only point where the terrain gave them a chance to prevail against the odds. Sherman kept moving. He reached Brandon the following evening — his forty-fourth birthday — and Morton on the 9th. In less than a week, he had not only covered better than half the distance between Vicksburg and Meridian; he had also scattered his opposition so effectively that now there was nothing between him and his initial objective except one badly rattled gray division, in flight from the four blue ones in its rear.

He pressed on, spurred by fear that he would be late for his rendezvous with Smith, who was due to reach Meridian tomorrow, after ten days on the road. The march was single column now, to provide a more compact defense against Lee's still-probing horsemen, and while McPherson paused for a day of destructive work on the railroad around Morton, Hurlbut made such good time that by sundown of the 12th he had passed through Decatur, northeast of Newton Station, and was less than thirty miles from Meridian. Sherman decided to wait there for McPherson, who was expected within a couple of hours. Detaching a regiment from Hurlbut's rear to serve as a guard, he and his staff unsaddled their horses in the yard of a house where an aide had arranged for supper; after which the general lay down on a bed to get some sleep. He was awakened by shouts and shots, and looked out of a window to find butternut cavalry "dashing about in a cloud of dust, firing their pistols."

It developed that the colonel of the regiment detached to guard

★

him, mistaking a front-riding group of staff officers for the head of McPherson's column, had considered himself relieved and pushed on eastward in an attempt to overtake his division before dark. When Sherman learned that this was what had happened, he sent an aide to order the regiment back on the double, while he himself prepared to retire with his companions to a corncrib for a blockhouse-style defense. Fortunately, the rebel troopers were giving their attention to some straggler wagons, never suspecting the larger prize within their reach, and before the townspeople could call it to their attention, the red-faced colonel returned on the run and drove them off, delivering the army commander from the gravest personal danger he had experienced since his near capture at Collierville, four months ago yesterday. Presently McPherson did in fact come up, and Sherman went back to bed for a full night's sleep.

Another two days of marching brought the head of the blue column into Meridian by midafternoon of February 14. Polk had left by rail with the last of his troops that morning, retiring beyond the Tombigbee to Demopolis. After pleading in vain for reinforcements, he had concerned himself with the removal of an estimated $12,000,000 in military property, south to Mobile or east to Selma, together with the rolling stock of the three railroads; so that when Sherman marched in on Valentine's Day he found the warehouses yawning empty and the tracks deserted in all four directions.

Furious at the loss, he put the blame on Smith, who should have arrived four days ago, in time to prevent the removal of the spoils, but who had neither come himself nor sent a courier to account for his departure from the schedule he had agreed to, three weeks back, in Memphis. Determined to make the most of the situation as he found it — for though the military property had been hauled away, the facilities were still there, and there was civilian property in abundance — the red-haired Ohioan gave his men a well-earned day of rest, then distributed the tools he had brought along to assure the efficient accomplishment of the object of his raid. "For five days," he subsequently reported, "10,000 men worked hard and with a will in that work of destruction, with axes, crowbars, sledges, clawbars, and with fire, and I have no hesitation in pronouncing the work as well done. Meridian, with its depots, storehouses, arsenal, hospitals, offices, hotels, and cantonments, no longer exists."

While the rest of the soldiers in the two corps were attending to the railroads — Hurlbut north and east of town, McPherson south and west, burning trestles, smashing culverts, and warping rails over bonfires fed by crossties — Sherman kept peering through the smoke for some sign of Smith and his 7000 troopers, who were to lead the march on Selma as soon as the present demolition work was finished. But there was none.

"It will be a novel thing in war," he complained testily, between puffs on a cigar, "if infantry has to await the motions of cavalry."

Members of the 35th New Jersey Infantry pose in the short jackets and sashes typical of a Zouave unit. The unit was part of McPherson's XVII Corps during Sherman's drive on Meridian, Mississippi.

★ ★ ★   is impatience was due in large part to the disappointing contrast between his present situation, in which the nonarrival of his cavalry left him marking time in Meridian — albeit vigorously, to a tempo set by pounding sledges and crackling flames — and the prospect that had seemed to lie before him, three weeks ago in Memphis, at the time of his conference with the commander of the mounted column. Smith not only had been eager to undertake the assignment, but had shown a ready appreciation of what was required to make it a success. He was to ride southeast to Okolona, visiting such destruction upon the inhabitants of this 100-mile swath across North Mississippi as his schedule would permit, and then turn south along the Mobile & Ohio, scourging the heart of

★

the Black Prairie region with fire and sword, all the way to his projected link-up with the infantry, another 130 miles below, for the combined march eastward across the Tombigbee. As for the tactical danger, the cavalryman declared that the best procedure would be "to pitch into Forrest wherever I find him." He did not say this boastfully, but rather in accordance with his instructions, which advised him to do just that.

Neither a greenhorn nor a braggart, Smith was a West Pointer like his commander and fellow Ohioan, who was ten years his senior, and had risen on ability in the army to which he returned on the outbreak of war, interrupting what had promised to be (and later was) a distinguished career as a civil engineer. Graduating with Sheridan and McPherson, he had commanded a brigade at Shiloh while these other two Ohioans were still low-ranking staffers, and he led a division with such proficiency throughout the Vicksburg campaign that Grant soon afterwards made him his chief of cavalry. What was more, in the case of his present assignment, his confidence in his combat-tested ability as a leader was greatly strengthened by a look at the composition of the force he would be leading.

In addition to five regiments he brought with him from Middle Tennessee, he would have at his disposal a Memphis-based division under Ben Grierson, who had ridden to fame over nearly the same route nine months before, and a veteran brigade already ordered to join him from Union City, up near the Kentucky line. Out of this total of better than 12,000 cavalry, he would select the 7000 he was to have in his hard-riding column, armed to a man with breech-loading carbines and accompanied by twenty pieces of artillery, double-teamed for speed. This would give him not only three times as many guns and twice as many troopers as were with Forrest, whose newly recruited division was all that stood between Smith and his objective, but also the largest and best-equipped body of Federal horsemen ever assembled in the western theater. It was small wonder he expressed no doubt that he could accomplish all that was asked of him at the late-January conference.

But Sherman had no sooner gone downriver than Smith learned that the 2000-man brigade from Union City, nearly one third of his intended force, was being delayed by floods and washouts all along the way. "Exceedingly chagrined," he informed the army commander that he thought it "wisest, best, and most promising" to postpone his departure until the brigade's arrival brought his column up to the strength assured him beforehand. He still felt "eager to pitch into [Forrest]," he said, "but I know that it is not your desire to 'send a boy to the mill.' " This was written on February 2, the day after he was supposed to have left Collierville and the day before Sherman left Vicksburg. As it turned out, moreover, the brigade did not reach Memphis until the 8th, and Smith found its horses so worn by their exertions that he felt obliged to give them a two-day rest. Then at last, on February 11 — one day after he was to have reached his initial objective, 230 miles away — he set out. He would "push ahead with all energy," he declared in a follow-up dispatch to Sherman, reporting that his men and their mounts were "in splendid condition" for the rigorous march. "Weather beautiful; roads getting good," he added.

In a companion message to Grant, however, he sounded less ebullient. Earlier he had informed the department commander that his troopers were "well in hand, well provided with everything, and eager for the work," but now he confessed that the last-minute delay — already prolonged one day beyond the ten he was to have spent riding southward for the link-up at Meridian — had been "so long and so vexatious that I have worried myself into a state of morbid anxiety, and fear that I will be entirely too late to perform my part of the work."

Even though he was traversing, southeast of Collierville, what one of his lieutenants called a "rough, hopeless, God-forsaken" country, despoiled by nearly two years of contention and hard-handed occupation, his spirits rose in the course of the early stages of the march, partly because the tension of waiting had finally been relieved and partly because his prediction that Forrest would "show fight between the Coldwater and the Tallahatchie" was not borne out. He crossed the former stream near Holly Springs on the 12th and the latter at New Albany two days later — simultaneously, although he did not know it, with Sherman's arrival in Meridian — "without firing a shot." By now the column was badly strung out, however, and he was obliged to call a halt while the rear elements caught up; with the result that he did not reach Okolona until February 18. His schedule required a march rate of about twenty-five miles a day, but in this first week he had not averaged half that, despite the fact that he had encountered no opposition more formidable than a "rabble of State troops" near Pontotoc, which he brushed aside with ease, and had spent little time on the destructive work that was so much a part of his assignment. This last was because, so far, all he had run across that was worth destroying were a few outlying barns and gins. Now that he was astride the M&O, however, the opportunity for such labor was considerably enlarged: so much so, indeed, that from Okolona to West Point, a distance of about thirty miles, his troopers spent more time ripping up track and setting fires than they did in the saddle. "During two days," a brigade commander later wrote, "the sky was red with the flames of burning corn and cotton."

The sky was red with more flames than these; for the blue horsemen — especially those who were off on their own, as stragglers or outriders; "bummers," they would be called a bit later in the conflict — did not neglect the chance to scorch the holdings of secessionists in their path. What was more, a Federal colonel added, slaves on plantations roundabout, "driven wild with the infection, set the torch to mansion houses, stables, cotton gins, and quarters," and "came en masse to join our column, leaving only fire and absolute destruction behind them." Smith, for one, was "deeply pained" to find his command "disgraced by incendiarism of the most shocking kind. I have ordered the first man caught in the act to be shot," he notified Grierson, "and I have offered $500 reward for his detection." As for the Negroes, though he had encouraged them to join him as a means of increasing the disruption of the region and decreasing its future contribution to the Confederate war effort, he now had some 3000 of them on his hands and was finding them a severe encumbrance to his so-called "flying column," just at a time when he seemed likely to have to move his fastest. Despite his relief that Forrest had failed to "show fight" in the early stages of the march, it had begun to occur to him that the Tennessean might be postponing his attack until he reached a position "where he could concentrate a larger force, and where we would be to some extent jaded and farther from home."

By way of confirmation for these fears, a recently captured Indiana trooper managed to escape and rejoin his outfit on February 19, south of Okolona, with information that "Forrest's whole force was reported to be in the

> *It seemed to him that his adversary,*
> *with the unexpected advantage of*
> *superior numbers, was laying a trap*
> *for him just down the line.*

vicinity of West Point," barely a dozen miles ahead, and was "said to be 8000 or 9000 strong." Consequently when his lead elements ran into stiffer resistance next morning in that direction, Smith paused for thought. It seemed to him that his adversary, with the unexpected advantage of superior numbers, was laying a trap for him just down the line. He thought about this long and hard, and that evening his adjutant replied to a dispatch from one of his brigade commanders: "The general is very sick tonight."

His information was partly wrong, but his conclusion was entirely right. Though Forrest had a good deal less than half the number of men reported by the slippery Hoosier, he was indeed laying a trap for the blue column moving toward him down the Mobile & Ohio: a trap whose springing, incidentally, would commit his green command to its first concerted action. He had come to Mississippi in mid-November with fewer than 300 veterans from his old brigade, and two weeks later he took them northward, deep into West Tennessee, on a month-long tour of recruiting duty behind the Union lines, from which he returned by New Year's with some 3500

Encouraged to run away from slavery, blacks mingle with and aid Federal soldiers of Sherman's rear guard in this scene from Harper's Weekly.

effectives, a sizable drove of hogs and cattle, and forty wagonloads of bacon.

As here applied, the term "effectives" was questionable, however, since his recruits were mostly absentees and deserters, men who had skedaddled at least once before and could be expected to do so again at the first chance. "Forrest may cavort about that country as much as he pleases," Sherman had said when he heard what the rebel cavalryman was up to, north of Memphis. "Every conscript they now catch will cost a good man to watch." That this was a quite reasonable assertion no one knew better than the newly promoted major general who had this jumpy, unarmed mass in charge. But he depended on rigorous training and stern discipline — along with a few summary executions, if they were what was needed — to discourage the fulfillment of the Ohioan's prediction; after which would come the fighting that would knit what he now referred to as "my force of raw, undrilled, and undisciplined troops" into a cohesive unit, stamped with the aggressive personality of its leader and filled with a fierce pride in itself and him. With this in mind, he began in early January a program of unrelenting drill, mounted and dismounted, combined with a system of sharp-eyed inspections to assure compliance with his directives.

This had been in progress barely a month when he received word at his headquarters, north of Panola, that Sherman was on the march from Vicksburg, 150 miles to the south, evidently intending to strike at Meridian and possibly also at Selma or Mobile. Eight days later, Smith left Collierville, 50 miles to the north, and Forrest made this second column his concern, determined to prevent a junction of the two, though even the smaller one had twice his strength and was infinitely superior in experience and equipment.

While Smith was moving southeast, from Holly Springs to Okolona, Forrest paralleled the blue march by shifting from Panola to Starkville. Outnumbered two to one, he could not risk an all-out attack in open country; nor could he lie in wait for the invaders until he knew where they were headed and what route they would take to get there. They might, for example, cross the Tombigbee east of Tupelo for a link-up with Sherman at Demopolis or Selma, leaving the graybacks crouched in a useless ambush far behind, or they might turn abruptly southwest and make for Jackson, passing in rear of the butternut column hurrying eastward. So Forrest bided his time and awaited developments, keeping his four undersized brigades spread out to counter an advance from any one of several directions. Then on February 19, when Smith began his wrecking descent of the M&O, it was plain that he intended to follow the railroad all the way to Meridian, and Forrest was free to develop a specific plan to stop him.

Which he did. Sending one brigade to West Point as a bait to lure the bluecoats on, he ordered the others to take up a position three miles below, in a swampy pocket enclosed on the west and south by Sakatonchee and Oktibbeha creeks and on the east by the Tombigbee. That was the trap. The bait brigade, commanded by Colonel Jeffrey Forrest, the general's twenty-six-year-old brother, fell back next day as ordered, skirmishing lightly to draw the Federals through West Point and into the pocket prepared for their destruction. They followed cautiously, into and just beyond the town; but there they stopped, apparently for the night. Believing that they would come on again next morning, February 21, Forrest continued his preparations to receive them with a double envelopment.

He was wrong. Although there was an advance, which brought on a brief engagement, it soon became evident that this was a mere feint — a rear-guard action, designed to cover a withdrawal. Nearly two thirds of the way to his objective, Smith had given up trying to reach it; had decided, instead, to backtrack. Ahead were swamps and an enemy force reported to be larger than his own, while he was already ten full days behind schedule, still with eighty-odd miles to go and some 3000 homeless Negroes on his hands. "Under the circumstances," he afterwards declared, "I determined not to move my encumbered command into the trap set for me by the rebels."

Forrest, having gained what he called the "bulge," reacted fast. If the Yankees would not come to him, then he would go to them. And this he did, with a vengeance. Being, as he said later, "unwilling they should leave the country without a fight," he ordered his entire command to take up the pursuit of the retreating bluecoats. Moreover, the rear-guard skirmish had no sooner begun than he attended to another matter of grave concern: namely, the behavior of his "raw, undrilled, and undisciplined" troopers in their reaction to being shot at, many of them for the first time. As he approached the firing line he met a panic-stricken Confederate stumbling rearward, hatless and gunless, in full flight from his first taste of combat. Forrest dismounted to intercept him, flung him face-down by the roadside, then took up a piece of brush and administered what a startled witness described as "one of the worst thrashings I have ever seen a human being get." This done, he jerked the unfortunate soldier to his feet, faced him about, and gave him a shove that sent him stumbling in the direction of the uproar he had fled from. "Now, God damn you, go back to the front and fight!" he shouted after him. "You might as well be killed there as here, for if you ever run away again you'll not get off so easy."

Still raw and undrilled, but by no means undisciplined, the man rejoined his comrades on the firing line, and the story quickly spread, not only through the division — as the general no doubt intended — but also through both armies, until finally it was made the subject of a *Harper's Weekly* illustration titled "Forrest Breaking in a Conscript."

For the next two days he handled Smith in much the same fashion. After driving the rear-guard Federals through West Point, he came upon them again, three miles beyond the town, stoutly posted along a timbered ridge approachable only by a narrow causeway. His solution was to send one regiment

William Sooy Smith was chief of cavalry for the Federal Army of the Tennessee during the Meridian campaign.

galloping wide around the enemy flank, with orders to strike the rear, while the others dismounted to attack in front. Admittedly, this was a lot to ask of green troops, but Forrest employed a method of persuasion quite different from the one he had used a while ago on the panicked conscript. "Come on, boys!" he roared, and led the way, thus setting an example which caused one of his men to recall, years later, that "his immediate presence seemed to inspire everyone with his terrible energy, more like that of a piece of powerful steam machinery than of a human being." So led, they drove the bluecoats from the ridge, then re-mounted and continued the pursuit until nightfall, when their commander called a halt, midway between West Point and Okolona, in a hastily abandoned bivouac area, stocked not only with rations and forage, but also with wood for the still-burning campfires.

While the graybacks bedded down and slept beside the cozy warmth provided by their foes, Smith kept his main body plodding northward and did not stop until well past midnight, within four miles of Okolona. Burdened with captured stock and runaway slaves, and weary as they were from their long march — since sunup, they had covered better than twice the distance they had managed on any one of the other nine days since they left Collierville — his men got a late start next morning. By that time Forrest, who had had his troop-ers up and on the go by dawn, well rested and unencumbered, had closed the ten-mile gap and was snapping again at the tail and flanks of the blue column.

Smith was learning, as Streight had learned before him, that it could be even more dangerous to run from the Tennessean than it was to stand and fight him. However, instead of turning on him with all he had, he dropped off a

★

couple of regiments just beyond Okolona and a full brigade at Ivey's Hill, five miles farther along on the road to Pontotoc, still intent on saving his train and protecting the Negroes in his charge. After a running fight through the town, hard on the heels of the rear guard, the gray pursuers came upon the first of these two prepared positions and were brought to a halt by fire from the superior Federal weapons. At this point Forrest arrived. "Where is the enemy's whole position?" he asked Colonel Tyree Bell, whose brigade had the lead this morning. "You see it, General," Bell replied, and added: "They are preparing to charge." "Then we will charge them," Forrest said: and did.

The result was a blue rout. Five guns were abandoned shortly thereafter by an artillery lieutenant who complained hotly in his report that his battery had been forced off the road and into a ditch by Union troopers who overtook him "in perfect confusion," hallooing: "Go ahead, or we'll be killed!" The chase continued to Ivey's Hill, where the defenders, allowed more time to get set, gave a considerably better account of themselves. Opening ranks to let the fugitives through, they took under well-aimed fire the two brigades advancing toward them across the prairie.

At the first volley the commanders of both were shot, one in the hand, the other through the throat. The second of these was Jeffrey Forrest, and though the general reached him immediately after he fell — this youngest of his five brothers, posthumously born and sixteen years his junior, whom he had raised as a son and made into a soldier — he found him dead. He remained bent over him for a minute or two, then rose and ordered his bugler to sound the charge. The fighting that followed was savage and hand-to-hand. Within the next hour, Forrest had two horses killed under him and accounted in person for three enemy soldiers, shot or sabered.

Thus assailed, the Federals once more fell back to try another stand in a position ten miles from Pontotoc; which was also lost, along with another gun, but which at any rate ended the relentless chase that had begun two days ago, nearly fifty miles away, below West Point. "Owing to the broken down and exhausted condition of men and horses, and being almost out of ammunition," Forrest presently reported, "I was compelled to stop pursuit." Smith was unaware of this, however, and kept going even harder than before. Judging the rebel strength by Forrest's aggressiveness, he believed that Stephen Lee had arrived to join the chase, though in point of fact he now had nothing on his trial but the "rabble of state troops" he had brushed aside when he passed this way the week before, headed in the opposite direction. In Pontotoc by midnight, he resumed the march at 3 a.m. and cleared New Albany that afternoon, February 23, destroying in his rear the bridges across the Tallahatchie. All next day he kept moving, unwilling to risk another stand, and rode at last into Collierville on the 25th, having covered in five days the same distance he had required ten days to cover while going south. Not even then did he call a halt, however; he kept going all the following day, through Germantown to Memphis, there ending at last what one brigade commander described as "a weary, disheartened, almost panic-stricken flight, in the greatest disorder and confusion."

His loss in men had not been great (it amounted to 388 in all, including 155 missing, as compared to a total of 144 for his opponent — a disparity which Forrest, as the attacker, could only account for by "the fact that we kept so close to them that the enemy overshot our men") but the cost in horse-flesh had been cruel. Smith returned with no more than 2200 riders who could be described as adequately mounted; the other 4800 were either on foot or astride horses no longer fit for service in the field. A corresponding loss in cavalry morale, so lately on the rise in all the Union armies, was indicated by an unhappy colonel's remark that "the expedition filled every man connected with it with a burning shame."

Nor was that by any means the worst of it from the northern point of view. The worst was still to come, resulting not so much from Federal losses as from Confederate gains. Practically overnight, by this victory over twice their number — and the capture, in the process, of six guns and several stands of colors — Forrest's green recruits had acquired a considerable measure of that fierce pride which in time would enable their commander to prevail against even longer odds and for much larger stakes. Already he was preparing to go over to the offensive, beginning with a return to West Tennessee and the accomplishment there of a great deal more than the mere enlargement of his now veteran division.

★   ★   ★   Though Sherman had been doubtful of Smith's competence from the start, deeming him "too mistrustful of himself for a leader against Forrest," this took none of the sting from his censure of his fellow Ohioan for "allowing General Forrest to head him off and defeat him with an inferior force." But that was later, after he learned the gloomy particulars of the cavalry excursion, and in any case he had waited for Smith no longer than it took him to wipe the appointed meeting place off the map. By the time the frazzled horsemen returned to Memphis, Sherman had recrossed the Pearl and gone into bivouac at Canton, north of Jackson, still with no knowledge of what, if anything, had happened to the mounted column, which in fact had begun its retreat from West Point on the day he ended his five-day stay in Meridian and abandoned his proposed advance on Selma.

Not that he considered his own part in the campaign anything less than "successful in the highest degree," both on the outward march and the return, which he made along a different route, twenty-odd miles to the north, so as to avoid the grainless, cowless, hogless trail his twelve brigades of infantry had blazed while slogging eastward. "My movement to Meridian stampeded all

Alabama," he informed Halleck three days later, on February 29. "Polk retreated across the Tombigbee and left me to smash things at pleasure, and I think it is well done. . . . We broke absolutely and effectually a full hundred miles of railroad . . . and made a swath of desolation fifty miles broad across the State of Mississippi which the present generation will not forget." After listing his spoils, which included "some 500 prisoners, a good many refugee families, and about ten miles of negroes," he announced that the destruction he had wrought "makes it simply impossible for the enemy to risk anything but light cavalry this side of Pearl River; consequently, I can reduce the garrisons of Memphis, Vicksburg, and Natchez to mere guards, and, in fact, it will set free 15,000 men for other duty. I could have gone on to Mobile or over to Selma," he added, "but without other concurrent operations it would have been unwise." Privately, however, in a companion letter to his wife, he confessed his regret that Smith's nonarrival had prevented him from applying what his foes were calling "the Sherman torch" to Alabama. "As it was," he chuckled, for he always enjoyed a small joke on the clergy, "I scared the bishop out of his senses."

It was Polk he meant, of course, and he was right; the bishop had indeed been frightened, not only for Meridian, Demopolis, and Selma, but also for Mobile, a greater prize than any of those others in his care. His fears for the Confederacy's only remaining Gulf port east of the Mississippi had been enlarged in late January when Farragut — who had just returned from a New York holiday, taken while the *Hartford* was being refitted in the Brooklyn Navy Yard — appeared before the place with a squadron of multigunned warships, evidently intending to launch another of his all-out attacks, not one of which had ever failed with him on hand to see that it was pressed to the required extremity. In point of fact, the admiral was only there to heighten Polk's fears for the loss of the port and to discourage him from drawing reinforcements from its garrison when Sherman began his march. There was no need to attack; he accomplished his purpose merely by his month-long presence, just outside the bay, and gained in the process much valuable information which he would put to substantial use when he came back again, not for a feint or diversion, but in earnest. As a result, when Sherman set out from Vicksburg in early February, Polk was convinced that his goal was Mobile and that what was intended was a combined assault, by land and water, designed to remove that vital port from the list of the South's assets in continuing its struggle to maintain its national existence. Outnumbered two to one, or worse, the bishop called loudly on Richmond for assistance, and Richmond passed his appeal to Johnston, the only possible source for reinforcements in a hurry. Whereupon there was staged in North Georgia a grim comedy involving a balking contest between the two commanders, blue and gray.

Johnston protested for all he was worth. In the first place, he did not believe the proposed reinforcements could reach Polk in time to head off Sherman; and what was more he was convinced that any substantial reduction of his already outnumbered force, which was being required to maintain a position that had "neither intrinsic strength nor strategic advantage," would not only expose Atlanta to capture by the blue mass in his front, but would also be likely to result in the destruction of what would remain of the army charged with its defense. This chilling presentation to the government of a choice between losing one or the other of two of its principal cities had the effect of delaying, though not of forestalling, a peremptory order requiring the immediate detachment of Hardee's corps to Polk for the purpose of covering Mobile. Received on February 16, the order began to be carried out four days later — by coincidence, on the day Sherman began his return march from Meridian — when the three divisions boarded the cars at Dalton for the long ride to Demopolis. Arriving next day they found they were unneeded; Sherman had withdrawn. Polk put them promptly back aboard the cars to rejoin Johnston, who by now was sending up distress signals of his own.

His worst fears had been realized; Thomas was advancing. The Union-loyal Virginian had also received peremptory orders, and he too had delayed their execution. Instructed on February 14 to make a "formidable reconnaissance" of Johnston's position, he took a week to get ready, then started forward from Ringgold on the eighth day, February 22, two days after Hardee departed with the divisions under Cheatham, Walker, and Cleburne. Grant's hope was that Thomas would catch his adversary off balance and thus be able to drive him back from Rocky Face Ridge and beyond Dalton, in order to "get possession of the place and hold it as a step toward a spring campaign."

With three of his seven divisions 350 roundabout miles away, Johnston was something worse than merely off balance when Thomas moved against him. Palmer's corps made the opening thrust at Tunnel Hill. Formerly occupied by Cleburne, this western spur of Rocky Face Ridge was now held only by Wheeler, whose horse artillery raised such a clatter that the bluecoats were discouraged from attacking until the following day, February 24. By then the rebel troopers had fallen back through Buzzard Roost Gap to cover the flanks of the infantry disposed along the ridge. Thomas probed the passes on the 25th, making some progress against the wide-spread defenders — especially at Dug Gap, immediately southwest of Dalton — but when Palmer launched a coördinated assault next morning he found that Hardee's three divisions, having completed their round-trip journey to Demopolis, were in position on the ridge; Cleburne, in fact, was on the flank of the flankers. Accordingly, Thomas withdrew as he had come, returning to Ringgold on the same day Sooy Smith rode back into Memphis and Sherman descended on Canton. His "formidable reconnaissance" had cost him 345 casualties and had failed in its larger purpose of seizing Dalton "as a step toward a spring campaign"; but he, like Farragut outside

Mobile, had learned much that would be useful when he returned in earnest.

As for Johnston, he was agreeably surprised. He had expected to be thrown into precipitate retreat; whereas his men had not only maintained the integrity of a position which he declared had "little to recommend it," but had inflicted better than twice the 167 casualties they suffered. Even more heartening than the bare tactical result was the contrast between the army's present frame of mind, here on Rocky Face Ridge, and the one that had been evidenced a dozen weeks ago on Missionary Ridge. Unquestionably its spirit had been lifted: perhaps indeed a bit too much, at least in one respect, to suit Old Joe. For in congratulating his troops on their work, he was critical of the artillery officers for having "exhibited a childish eagerness to discharge their pieces."

By now the Confederates had returned to Meridian, or at any rate to the desolation Sherman had created in its place. Speaking in Jackson on his first western visit, just over a year ago, Jefferson Davis had warned that the invaders had it in mind to handle Mississippi "without gloves," and now his words had been borne out; Meridian was an example of what the men he referred to as

Federals near Ringgold (top) observe distant Confederate positions, and a sentry (bottom) guards the tracks in that town.

"worse than vandal hordes" could accomplish when their commander turned them loose with the admonition that "vigorous war . . . means universal destruction." In addition to the damage inflicted on the town itself, a total of twenty-four miles of railroad track, extending an average half dozen miles in all four directions, had been demolished, the crossties burned, the rails heated and twisted into what were known as "Sherman neckties." Beyond this circumference of utter destruction, for a distance of nearly fifty miles north and south, not a bridge or a trestle had been left unwrecked on the Mobile & Ohio. Already, in the course of their march from Jackson, the raiders had disposed of fifty-one bridges on the Southern, together with an even larger number of trestles and culverts, and they had extended their work eastward, nine miles beyond the junction, to add three more bridges and five trestles to the tally.

And yet, sad as it was to survey the charred remains of what once had passed for prosperity in this nonindustrial region, sadder by far were the people of those counties through which the blue column had slogged on its way to and from the town that now was little more than a scar on the green breast of earth. They had the stunned, unbelieving look of survivors of some terrible natural disaster, such as a five-day hurricane, a tidal wave, or an earthquake: with the underlying difference that their grief had been inflicted by human design and was in fact a deliberate product of a new kind of war, quite unlike the one for which they had bargained three years ago, back in that first glad springtime of secession. It was, moreover, a war that was still in progress, and somehow that was the strangest, most distressful aspect of all. Their deprivation was incidental to the large design. They were faced with the aftermath before the finish.

Polk took no such gloomy view of the prospect. Though he could scarcely deny the all-too-evident validity of Sherman's boast of having "made a swath of desolation fifty miles broad across the State of Mississippi which the present generation will not forget," he did not agree with his adversary's further assertion that the east-central portion of the state could be written off as a factor in the conflict. "I have already taken measures to have all the roads broken up by him rebuilt," the bishop notified Richmond two days after the raiders turned back in the direction they had come from, "and shall press that work vigorously." Press it he did. Summoning to his Demopolis headquarters President Samuel Tate of the Memphis & Charleston Railroad, he put him in general charge of the restoration, with full authority to requisition both property and labor. Tate was a driver. Despite a crippling shortage of rails and spikes — not to mention the inevitable objections of planters to the impressment of such of their Negroes as had not gone off with Smith and Sherman — within twenty-six days he had the Mobile & Ohio back in operation, from Tupelo south to Mobile Bay, along with the Alabama & Mississippi, from Meridian to the Tombigbee. The Southern took longer, mainly because of administrative complications, but within another five weeks it too was open, all the way to the Pearl.

But that was later. At the time he made it, February 28, Sherman's pronouncement: "My movement cleared Mississippi at one swoop, and with the railroad thus destroyed the Confederacy cannot maintain an army save cavalry west of Tombigbee," seemed to him irrefutable. He was back in Vicksburg by then, having come on ahead of the infantry, which he left marking time in Canton, as he said afterwards, "with orders to remain till about the 3d of March" — he was still hoping Sooy Smith would turn up — "and then come into Vicksburg leisurely." Pleased by the added destruction of several miles of the Mississippi Central, north of Jackson — together with 19 locomotives, 28 cars, and 724 carwheels, which helped to ease his disappointment that Polk had managed to save the rolling stock on the other roads within his reach — he proudly announced: "Everything with my command was successful in the highest degree."

That this was hardly an overstatement was evidenced by the anguished protests of his opponents and victims, soldiers and civilians, some of whom reported the damage at a larger figure than his own. Stephen Lee, for one, charged the raiders with "burning 10,000 bales of cotton and 2,000,000 bushels of corn and carrying off 8000 slaves, many mounted on stolen mules." He estimated the over-all loss at five million dollars, of which "three fourths was private property," and asked rhetorically: "Was this the warfare of the nineteenth century?"

Sherman was not inclined to dispute the statistics, and he had already given his answer to Lee's question. This was indeed the warfare of the nineteenth century, at any rate as he intended to practice it, and he was not only proud of what had been accomplished by this first large-scale application of the methods that had aroused the South Carolinian's moral indignation; he was also looking forward to the time when he could apply those methods elsewhere, perhaps even in the angry young cavalryman's native state, where the provocation had begun.

First though would come Georgia; Mississippi had been something of a warm-up, a practice operation in this regard, just as perhaps Georgia in turn would be a warm-up for the Carolinas. In any case Sherman had composed at Vicksburg, by way of further preparation while waiting to set out across Mississippi, a letter to the assistant adjutant general of his army, most of whose members were in camps around Chattanooga waiting for him to return from his current excursion and lead them against Joe Johnston and Atlanta. Ostensibly addressed to Major R. M. Sawyer, the letter was in fact a warning to the civilians in his southward path, as well as a legalistic justification for military harshness, since it dealt primarily with his intention regarding "the treatment of inhabitants known or suspected to be hostile or 'secesh.' " His policy up to now, he said, had been to leave the question to local commanders of occupation forces, "but [I] am willing to give them the benefit of my acquired knowledge and experience,"

These men of the 17th Ohio Infantry
participated in Thomas's initial moves on
Tunnel Hill and Buzzard Roost Gap.

and though he admitted that it was "almost impossible to lay down rules" for their guidance in such matters, he proceeded to do precisely that, and more.

"In Europe, whence we derive our principles of war, as developed by their histories," he began, "wars are between kings or rulers, through hired armies, and not between peoples. These remain as it were neutral, and sell their produce to whatever army is in possession. . . . Therefore the rule was, and is, that wars are confined to the armies and should not visit the homes of families or private interests." Little or none of this applied in the present instance, however, any more than it had done in the case of the Irish insurrection against William and Mary, who dispossessed the rebels of their property, sent them forthwith into exile, and gave their lands to Scottish emigrants. The same could be done with justice here, Sherman declared, but he preferred to withhold such measures for a time, on grounds that the guilt was not entirely restricted to the guilty. "For my part," he explained, "I believe this war is the result of false political doctrine, for which we all as a people are responsible . . . and I would give all a chance to reflect and when in error to recant. . . . I am willing to bear in patience that political nonsense of slave rights, States rights, freedom of conscience, freedom of the press, and such other trash as have deluded the Southern people into war, anarchy, bloodshed, and the foulest crimes that have disgraced any time or any people." He would bear all this in patience, but only for a season; meanwhile he would have the occupation commanders "assemble the inhabitants and explain to them these plain, self-evident propositions, and tell them that it is now for them to say whether they and their children shall inherit the beautiful land which by the accident of nature had fallen to their share." After this, if they persisted in the error of their ways, would come the thunder. "If they want eternal war, well and good; we accept the issue, and will dispossess them and put our friends in their places." Moreover, the longer they delayed recanting, the sterner their fate would be. "Three years ago, by a little reflection and patience, they could have had a hundred years of peace and prosperity, but they preferred war; very well. Last year they could have saved their slaves, but now it is too late. All the powers of earth cannot return to them their slaves, any more than their dead grandfathers. Next year their lands will be taken; for in war we can take them, and rightfully, too, and in another year they may beg in vain for their lives."

He warmed as he wrote, assuming the guise of an avenging angel — even the Archangel Michael — to touch on eschatology in the end. "To those who submit to the rightful law and authority, all gentleness and forbearance; but to the petulant and persistent secessionists, why, death is mercy, and the quicker he or she is disposed of the better. Satan and the rebellious saints of Heaven were allowed a continuous existence in hell merely to swell their just punishment. To such as would rebel against a Government so mild and just as ours was in peace, a punishment equal would not be unjust."

A copy went to his senator brother, with the request that it be printed for all to read, along and behind the opposing lines of battle. "Its publication would do no harm," he said, "except to turn the Richmond press against me as the prince of barbarians." Actually he was of the opinion that it would do much good, especially Southward, and he urged his adjutant to see that his views were presented to "some of the better people" of the region already occupied, with the suggestion that they pass them along to friends in whose direction he would be moving in the spring. "Read to them this letter," he wrote, "and let them use it so as to prepare them for my coming."

★   ★   ★

★

Shelby Foote

*Federal soldiers, guarding the
approaches to Washington, D.C.,
lounge around on Mason's Island,
across the Potomac from the
Georgetown section of the city.*

F O U R

Lincoln-Davis, a Final Contrast

1864 ★ ★ ★ ★ ★ ★ **Sherman's notion of how the war could be won was definite enough,** but whether it would be fought that way — with stepped-up harshness, to and through the finish — depended in no small measure on who would be directing it from the top. This was a presidential election year; the armies might have a new Commander in Chief before the advent of the victory which not even the ebullient Ohioan, in his days of highest feather, predicted would occur within the twelve-month span that lay between his return from Meridian, having demonstrated the effectiveness of his method, and the inauguration of the winner of the November contest at the polls. Moreover, the Republican convention was barely three months off, and though Lincoln had expressed a cautious willingness to stand for reëlection — "A second term would be a great honor and a great labor," he had told Elihu Washburne in October, "which together, perhaps, I would not decline if tendered" — whether he would be renominated appeared doubtful. For one thing, recent tradition was against it; none of the other eight Presidents since Andrew Jackson had served beyond a single term. Besides, whatever his popularity with the people, the men who controlled the convention seemed practically unanimous in their conviction that a better candidate could be found. "Not a Senator can be named as favorable to Lincoln's renomina-

★

tion," the Detroit *Free Press* had reported, and the claim went uncontradicted.

Nor was this opinion limited to his enemies. David Davis, who had managed his 1860 nomination, and who had been duly rewarded with a seat on the Supreme Court, declared in private: "The politicians in and out of Congress, it is believed, would put Mr Lincoln aside if they dared." Lyman Trumbull, an associate from early days and now a power in the Senate, believed however that it was not so much a question of daring as of tactics. Writing to a constituent back in Illinois, he presented the reasons behind this opposition and suggested that those who held them were merely biding their time between now and early June, when the delegates would convene in Baltimore. "The feeling for Mr Lincoln's re-election *seems* to be very general," he said, "but much of it I discover is only on the surface. You would be surprised, in talking with public men we meet here, to find how few, when you come to get at their real sentiment, are for Mr Lincoln's re-election. There is a distrust and fear that he is too undecided and inefficient to put down the rebellion. You need not be surprised if a reaction sets in before the nomination, in favor of some man supposed to possess more energy and less inclination to trust our brave boys in the hands and under the leadership of generals who have no heart in the war. The opposition to Mr L. may not show itself at all, but if it ever breaks out there will be more of it than now appears."

It broke out sooner than expected, though not from an unpredictable direction, the source of the explosion being Salmon Chase, or at any rate the men around or behind him, who saw in the adverse reaction to the overlenient Amnesty Proclamation an opportunity too fruitful to be neglected. Chase had been sobered by the Cabinet crisis of mid-December, fourteen months ago, but renewed ambition apparently caused him to forget his extreme discomfort at that time. In any case, in an attempt to influence various state conventions soon to be in session, a group of the Secretary's friends banded together and sent out in early February a "strictly private" letter afterwards known as the Pomeroy Circular. So called because it was issued over the signature of the group chairman, Senator Samuel C. Pomeroy of Kansas, a prominent Jacobin and old-line abolitionist, the document charged that "party machinery and official influence are being used to secure the perpetuation of the present Administration," asserted that "those who believe in the interests of the country and of freedom demand a change in favor of vigor and purity," and then went on to present five main points all delegates would do well to bear in mind.

The first two were against Lincoln, whose reëlection was not only "practically impossible" but also undesirable, since under him "the war may continue to languish" and "the cause of human liberty, and the dignity of the nation, suffer proportionately." The third point found "the 'one-term principle' absolutely essential to the certain safety of our republican institutions." The final two were devoted to Chase, who not only had "more of the qualities needed in

★

*Despite the political turmoil that swirled about him,
Lincoln took time out to sit for this placid portrait
with his son, Tad, on February 9, 1864.*

a President during the next four years than are combined in any other candidate," but had developed, as well, "a popularity and strength . . . unexpected even to his warmest admirers." Finally, each recipient was urged to "render efficient aid by exerting yourself at once to organize your section of the country" and to enter into correspondence with the undersigned chairman "for the purpose either of receiving or imparting information."

Lincoln was told of the "strictly private" circular as soon as it appeared. On February 6, Ward Lamon wrote from New York that a prominent banker there had received in his mail that morning, under the frank of an Ohio congressman, "a most scurrilous and abominable pamphlet about you, your administration, and the succession." Copies arrived from other friends on the lookout, but got no farther than Nicolay's desk; Lincoln would not read them. "I have determined to shut my eyes, so far as possible, to everything of that sort," he explained. "Mr Chase makes a good Secretary, and I shall keep him

Chase out would be considerably more formidable than Chase in; Lincoln had no intention of accepting a resignation which, by splitting the party, might well lose the Republicans the election, whoever the candidate was.

where he is. If he becomes President, all right. I hope we shall never have a worse man." He knew, of course, of the Ohioan's machinations, which were strengthened by the dispensation of some ten thousand jobs in his department, and he said of his activities as an inside critic, "I suppose he will, like the bluebottle fly, lay his eggs in every rotten spot he can find." But to some who advised that the "perfidious ingrate" be fired he replied: "I am entirely indifferent to his success or failure in these schemes, so long as he does his duty at the head of the Treasury Department." To others he maintained that "the Presidential grub" had much the same effect on the Secretary as a horsefly had on a balky plow horse; he got more work out of him when he was bit.

Or perhaps it was even simpler than that. Perhaps Lincoln enjoyed watching the performance Chase gave. It was, after all, pretty much a repeat performance, and he already knew the outcome, agreeing beforehand with Welles, who predicted in his diary that the Pomeroy Circular would be "more dangerous in its recoil than its projectile." His adversaries had bided their time; now he was biding his. A Massachusetts congressman, returning from a visit to the White House at the height of this latest Chase-for-President boom, informed a colleague that Lincoln was only waiting for the Treasury chief to put himself a little more clearly in the wrong. "He thinks that Mr C. will sufficiently soon force the question. In the meantime I think he is wise in waiting till the pear is ripe."

The pear ripened over the weekend of Washington's Birthday. On Saturday, February 20, the *Constitutional Union* printed in full the text of the circular, and when it was picked up on Monday by the *National Intelligencer,* Chase could no longer pretend to be unaware of what his friends were doing in his behalf. Writing to Lincoln that same day, he declared however that he had "had no knowledge of the existence of this letter before I saw it in the *Union.*" Some weeks ago, he went on, "several gentlemen" had called on him "in connection with the approaching election of Chief Magistrate," and though he had not felt that he could forbid them to work as they chose, he had "told them distinctly that I could render them no help, except what might come incidentally from the faithful discharge of public duties, for these must have my whole time"; otherwise, he knew nothing of what had been done by these gentlemen. "I have thought this explanation due to you as well as to myself," he told Lincoln. "If there is anything in my action or position which in your judgment will prejudice the public interest in my charge, I beg you to say so. I do not wish to administer the Treasury Department one day without your entire confidence. For yourself," he continued, appending a sort of amiable tailpiece to his tentative resignation, "I cherish sincere respect and esteem; and, permit me to add, affection. Differences of opinion as to administrative action have not changed these sentiments; nor have they been changed by assaults upon me by persons who profess to spread representations of your views and policy. You are not responsible for acts not your own; nor will you hold me responsible except for what I do or say myself. Great numbers now desire your re-election. Should their wishes be fulfilled by the suffrages of the people, I hope to carry with me into private life the sentiments I now cherish, whole and unimpaired."

He received next day a one-sentence reply, as inconclusive as it was brief. "Yours of yesterday in relation to the paper issued by Senator Pomeroy was duly received; and I write this note merely to say I will answer a little more fully when I can find the leisure to do so. Yours truly, A. Lincoln."

Chase out would be considerably more formidable than Chase in; Lincoln had no intention of accepting a resignation which, by splitting the party, might well lose the Republicans the election, whoever the candidate was. He did wait six full days, however, before he found "the leisure" to compose his promised answer. This may have been done primarily to allow the Ohioan plenty of time to squirm, but it also afforded others a chance to contribute to the squirmer's discomfort by heating up the griddle. When Chase spoke of "assaults upon me by persons who profess to spread representations of your views," it was the Blairs he meant: specifically, Montgomery and Frank. Back in the fall, as

*Twice — in late
1862 and in early
1864 — Treasury Sec-
retary Salmon Chase
was caught in his
own political web and
pushed into resigna-
tion. Lincoln, want-
ing to keep an eye
on the savvy poli-
tician, refused both
attempts and kept
Chase in office.*

principal speaker at a Maryland rally, the Postmaster General had referred to the Jacobins as "co-adjutors of Presidential schemers," making it clear that he had the Treasury head in mind as the chief schemer, and since then he had been castigating his fellow Cabinet member at practically every opportunity. Even so, he was not as harsh in this regard as his brother Frank, the soldier member of the family of whom it was said, "When the Blairs go in for a fight they go in for a funeral." Soon after his corps went into winter quarters near Chattanooga, Frank Blair came to Washington as a Missouri congressman. This had required the surrender of his commission as a major general, but Lincoln had promised to take care of that. He wanted Blair to stand for Speaker of the House, a post at which so stout a fighter could be of even more use to the Administration than on the field of battle, and he agreed that if this did not work out he would restore the commission and Blair could return to his duties as a corps com- mander under Sherman. But the plan fell through. By the time the Missourian

★

reached the capital in early January, Indiana's Schuyler Colfax, strongly anti-Lincoln in persuasion, had been elected Speaker. Nevertheless, since his corps was still lying idle down in Tennessee, Blair took his seat and stayed on in Washington, alert for a chance to strike at the President's enemies and his own.

A chance was not long in coming. On February 5, the day the Pomeroy Circular began to go out across the land, Blair rose in the House to speak in defense of the Administration's policies on amnesty and reconstruction, opposition to which he declared had been "concocted for purposes of defeating the renomination of Mr Lincoln" in order to open the way for "rival aspirants." Everyone knew it was Chase he meant, and three weeks later, on February 27 — four days into the six allowed for squirming — he made the charge specific, along with several others. Referring to the circular, he said of the candidate favored therein: "It is a matter of surprise that a man having the instincts of a gentleman should remain in the Cabinet after the disclosure of such an intrigue against the one to whom he owes his position. [However] I suppose the President is well content that he should stay; for every hour that he remains sinks him in the contempt of every honorable mind." Beyond this, Blair asserted that "a more profligate administration of the Treasury Department never existed under any government," and that investigation would show that "the whole Mississippi Valley is rank and fetid with the frauds and corruptions of its agents . . . some of [whom] I suppose employ themselves in distributing that 'strictly private' circular which came to light the other day."

Such charges hurt badly. Damage to Chase's reputation was damage to his soul, and though he thought of himself as a scrupulous administrator of the nation's funds, he knew quite well that for political reasons he had made agents of men who could by no means be said to measure up to his own high standards. In any case — perhaps out of pity, for the punishment was heavy — Lincoln ended at least a part of the Secretary's torment, two days later, by declining his resignation. "On consideration," he declared, "I find there is really very little to say. My knowledge of Mr. Pomeroy's letter having been made *public* came to me only the day you wrote; but I had, in spite of myself, known of its *existence* several days before. I have not yet read it, and I think I shall not. I was not shocked or surprised by the appearance of the letter, because I had had knowledge of Mr. Pomeroy's committee, and of secret issues which I supposed came from it, and of secret agents who I supposed were sent out by it, for several weeks." He was saying here that if he could know so much of what was going on behind his back, Chase must have known about it, too, despite his fervent denial. However that might be, Lincoln continued, "I have known just as little of these doings as my friends have allowed me to know . . . and I assure you, as you have assured me, that no assault has been made upon you by my instigation or with my countenance." Then came the close, the answer he had promised: "Whether you shall remain at the head of the Treasury Department is a question which I will not allow myself to consider from any standpoint other than my judgment of the public service, and, in that view, I do not perceive occasion for a change."

Chase was both relieved and pained: relieved to learn that he would remain at his post, which the long wait had taught him to value anew by persuading him that he was about to lose it, and pained because, as he plaintively observed, "there was no response in [the President's] letter to the sentiments of respect and esteem which mine contained." All this was rather beside the original point, however. Welles's prediction as to the "recoil" of the Pomeroy maneuver had already been borne out, its principal effect having been to rally Lincoln's friends to his support.

And of these, as events had shown, there were many. By the time of his belated reply to Chase on Leap Year Day, no less than fourteen states, either by formal action of their legislatures or by delegates in convention, had gone on record in favor of a second term for the man in office. Among them were New Hampshire, where the Secretary had been born, Rhode Island, where his new son-in-law was supposedly in political control, and finally — unkindest cut — Ohio. In fact, Chase was advised by men from his home state to disentangle himself from the embarrassment into which his ambition had led him, and this he did in a letter to a Buckeye supporter, requesting that "no further consideration be given my name." He also made it clear, however, that he was only asking this from a sense of duty to the cause, which must not be endangered, even though he was still convinced that "as President I could take care of the Treasury better with the help of a Secretary than I can as Secretary without the help of a President. But our Ohio folks don't want me enough." There was the rub; there was what had given him his quietus. "I no longer have any political side," he presently was saying, "save that of my country, and there are multitudes who like me care little for men but everything for measures."

The upshot of this pose of "honorable disinterestedness," as one of the newspapers reprinting the letter called it, was a general impression that he was merely awaiting a more favorable chance to get back in the running. A member of the Pomeroy group referred to the withdrawal as "a word of declination diplomatically spoken to rouse [our] flagging spirits," and David Davis likened its author to Mr Micawber waiting for something to "turn up." Chase had dreamed too long and too grandly for those who knew him to believe that he had stopped, even though it had been demonstrated conclusively, twice over, that his dreams would not come true. "Mr Chase will subside as a presidential candidate after the nomination is made, not before," the chairman of the Republican National Committee remarked, while the New York *Herald* ventured a comparison out of nature: "The Salmon is a queer fish, very wary, often appearing to avoid the bait just before gulping it down."

★ ★ ★ W hether Chase continued to dream and scheme made little difference now, though; Lincoln — with the Ohioan's unintentional assistance — had the nomination cinched. The election, however, was quite another matter. Despite the encouragement Republicans could draw from their successes at the polls in the past season, the outcome of the contest in November would depend even more on military than on political events of the next eight months, through spring and summer and into fall. For one thing, the fighting would be expensive both in money and blood, and the voters, as the ones who would do the paying and the bleeding, were unlikely to be satisfied with anything less than continuous victory at such prices. The past year had been highly satisfactory in this regard; Vicksburg and Missionary Ridge, even Gettysburg and Helena, were accomplishments clearly worth their cost. But the new year had started no better than the old year had ended. Sherman's destruction of Meridian could scarcely be said to offset Meade's unhappy stalemate at Mine Run or Seymour's abrupt defeat at Olustee, let alone Kilpatrick's frustration outside Richmond or the drubbing Sooy Smith had suffered at Okolona or the unprofitable demonstration Thomas had attempted against Dalton. A good part of the trouble seemed to proceed from mismanagement at the top, and the critics were likely to hold the top man responsible: especially in light of the fact that he had had a direct hand in a good proportion of these failures, all of which had been undertaken with his permission and some of which had been launched against the judgment of those below him on the military ladder. Now a reckoning time was coming, when the voters would have their say.

Congress, too, would have to face the voters: enough of it, at any rate, for defeat to cost the party now in power its comfortable majority, the loss of which would involve the surrender of committee chairmanships, the say-so in how and by whom the conflict would be pressed, easy access to much the largest pork barrel the nation had ever known, and finally the seizure and distribution of such spoils as would remain, two or three years from now, when the South was brought to its knees and placed at the disposal of the winners of the election this November. With so much at stake, it was no wonder the congressmen were jumpy at the prospect.

Moreover, their nervousness was intensified by a presidential order, dated February 1, providing for the draft, on March 10, of "five hundred thousand men to serve for three years or during the war." This call for "500,000 more" — made necessary by the heavy losses in battle this past year, as well as by the pending expiration of the enlistments of those volunteers who had come forward, two and three years ago, with all the fervor Sumter and McClellan had aroused — was graphic evidence of what the campaigns about to open were expected to cost in blood and money, and as such it presented the electorate with a yardstick by which to measure the height and depth of victories and defeats. The former, then, had better be substantial if they were to count for much at the polls, and by the same token the latter had better be minor, especially if they were anything like the recent setbacks, which were so obviously the result of miscalculations at the top and for which the voters could take their revenge by the way they marked their ballots. With this danger in mind, the lawmakers had returned to considering the previously rejected bill providing for a revival of the grade of lieutenant general, which in turn would provide for a man at the top who, by a combination of professional training and proven ability in the field, could operate within a shrinking margin for error that was already too narrow for the amateur who had been in unrestricted control these past three years.

Although Congress had no power to name the officer to whom the promotion would go in the event the bill went through, it was understood that Grant was the only candidate for the honor. Besides, Lincoln would do the naming, and by now the Illinois general was as much his favorite as anyone's. Far from being resentful of what another in his place — Jefferson Davis, for example — would have considered an encroachment by the legislative branch, he welcomed the relief the bill proposed to afford him from a portion of his duties as Commander in Chief. Above all, he was prepared to welcome Grant, who had applied at Donelson, Vicksburg, and Chattanooga the victory formula Lincoln had been seeking all these years. Others had sought it too, of course, and like him they now believed they had found it in the western commander. So many of them had done so by now, in fact, that they had provoked the only doubts he had about the general's fitness for the post. Like his friend McClernand, Lincoln was thoroughly aware that this war would produce a military hero who eventually would take up residence in the White House, and Grant's appeal in this respect had already reached the stage at which he was being wooed by prominent members of both political parties. They knew a winner when they saw one, and so did Lincoln; and that was the trouble. Involved as he was at the time in disposing of Chase, he was not anxious to promote the interests of a more formidable rival, which was precisely what he would be doing if he brought Grant to Washington as general-in-chief.

Nor was that the only drawback. There might be another even more disqualifying. "When the Presidential grub once gets in a man, it hides well," Lincoln had said of himself, and he thought this might apply as well to Grant, whose generalship would scarcely be improved by the distractive gnawing of the grub. However, when he inquired in that direction about such political aspirations, he was told the general had said in January that he not only was not a candidate for any office, but that as a soldier he believed he had no right to discuss politics at all. Pressed further, he relented so far as to add that, once the war was over, he might indeed run for mayor of Galena — so that, if elected, he could have the

*Lady Liberty pins a medal on the uniform of Ulysses S.
Grant in this Harper's Weekly cover engraving, which
portrays the nation's thanks to the western hero.*

sidewalk put in order between his house and the railroad station. Lincoln could appreciate the humor in this (though not the unconscious irony which others would perceive a few years later, when this view of the primary use of political office would be defined as "Grantism") but he was not entirely satisfied. For one thing, that had been several weeks ago, before the would-be kingmakers had begun to fawn on Grant in earnest. Adulation might have turned his head.

So Lincoln called in a friend of Grant's and asked him point-blank if the general wanted to be President. The man not only denied this; he produced a letter in which Grant said flatly that he had no political interests whatever. No doubt the statement was similar to one he made about this time in a letter to another friend, in which he declared: "My only desire will be, as it has been, to whip out rebellion in the shortest way possible, and to retain as high a position in the army afterwards as the Administration then in power may think me suitable for." Clearly, if this had been honestly said, it had not been said by a man who nurtured political ambitions. Lincoln's doubts were allayed. If Congress opened the way by passing the bill, he would see that the promotion went to the general for whom it was obviously intended.

Relief in any form would be most welcome, for the strain of frustration these past three years had brought him all too often to the verge of exhaustion and absolute despair. There was, after all, a limit to how many Fredericksburgs and Chancellorsvilles, how many Gettysburgs and Chickamaugas, even how many Olustees and Okolonas a man could survive. Mostly, though, the strain resulted from the difficulty of measuring up to private standards which he defined for a visitor whose petition he turned down, saying: "I desire to so conduct the affairs of this Administration that if, at the end, when I come to lay down the reins of power, I have lost every other friend on earth, I shall at least have one friend left, and that friend shall be deep down inside of me." Public critics he could abide or ignore, even those who called him clod or tyrant, clown or monster — "What's the harm in letting him have his fling?" he remarked of one of the worst of these; "If he did not pitch into me, he would into some poor fellow he might hurt" — but the critic lodged in his own conscience was not so easily lived with or dismissed. Some men appeared to have little trouble muffling that self-critic: not Lincoln, who saw himself "chained here in this Mecca of office-seekers," like Prometheus to his rock, a victim of his own dark-souled nature. "You flaxen men with broad faces are born with cheer, and don't know a cloud from a star," he once told a caller who fit this description; "I am of another temperament."

It sometimes seemed to him, moreover, that each recovery from gloom was made at the cost of future resiliency. "Nothing touches the tired spot," he had confessed the year before, and lately he had come back to this expression. Returning from a horseback ride that had seemed to lift his spirits, he was urged by a companion to find more time for rest and relaxation. "Rest?" he said. He shook his head, as if the word was unfamiliar. "I don't know. . . . I suppose it is good for the body. But the tired part is *inside,* out of reach."

If Grant was the man who could bring this inner weariness some measure of relief, Lincoln was not only willing to call him East to try his hand; he intended to wait no longer, before he did so, than the time required by Congress to pass the necessary legislation.

★ ★ ★ Opposing the Federal war of conquest (for, rebellion or revolution, that was what it would have to come to if the North was going to win) the Confederacy was fighting for survival. This had been, and would continue to be, Davis's principal advantage over his opponent in their respective capacities as leaders of their two nations: that he did not have to persuade his people of the reality of a threat which had been only too apparent ever since the first blue-clad soldier crossed the Potomac, whereas Lincoln was obliged to invoke a danger that was primarily theoretic. In the event that the Union broke in two, democracy might or might not "perish from the earth," but there could be no doubt at all — even before Sherman created, by way of a preview, his recent "swath of desolation" across Mississippi's midriff — about what would happen to the South if its bid for independence failed. However, this was only one face of a coin whose down side bore the inscription *States Rights.* Flip the coin and the advantage passed to Lincoln.

By suspending *habeas corpus,* or by ignoring at will such writs as the courts issued, the northern President kept his left hand free to deal as harshly as he pleased with those who sought to stir up trouble in his rear. It was otherwise with Davis. Denied this resource except in such drastic instances as the insurrection two years ago in East Tennessee, he had to meet this kind of trouble with that hand fettered. Often he had claimed this disadvantage as a virtue, referring by contrast to the North as a land where citizens were imprisoned "in utter defiance of all rights guaranteed by the institutions under which they live." Now though, with the approach of the fourth spring of the war, obstruction and defeatism had swollen to such proportions that conscription could scarcely be enforced or outright traitors prosecuted, so ready were hostile judges to issue writs that kept them beyond the reach of the authorities. Davis was obliged to request of Congress that it permit him to follow procedures he had scorned. "It has been our cherished hope," he declared in a special message on February 3, "that when the great struggle in which we are engaged was past we might exhibit to the world the proud spectacle of a people . . . achieving their liberty and independence, after the bloodiest war of modern times, without a single sacrifice of civil right to military necessity. But it can no longer be doubted that the zeal with which the people sprang to arms at the beginning of the contest has, in some parts of the Confederacy, been impaired by the long continuance and magnitude of the struggle. . . . Discontent, disaffection, and disloyalty are manifested among those who, through the sacrifices of others, have enjoyed quiet and safety at home. Public meetings have been held, in some of which a treasonable design is masked by a pretense of devotion to State sovereignty, and in others is openly avowed. . . . Secret leagues and associations are being formed. In certain localities, men of no mean position do not hesitate to avow their hostility to our cause and their advocacy of peace on the terms of submission."

All this was painful to admit, even in secret session, but Davis foresaw still greater problems unless the trend was checked. "Disappointment and despondency will displace the buoyant fortitude which animates [our brave soldiers] now. Desertion, already a frightful evil, will become the order of the day." He knew how sacred to his hearers the writ was, and he assured them that he would not abuse the license he was asking them to grant him. "Loyal citizens will not feel the danger, and the disloyal must be made to fear it. The very existence of extraordinary powers often renders their exercise unnecessary." In any case, he asserted in conclusion, "to temporize with disloyalty in the midst of war is but to quicken it to the growth of treason. I therefore respectfully recommend that the privilege of the writ of *habeas corpus* be suspended."

After twelve days of acrimonious debate — highlighted by an impassioned protest from the Vice President, who sent word from Georgia that if Davis was given the power he sought, "constitutional liberty will go down, never to rise again on this continent" — Congress agreed, though with profound misgivings, to a six-month suspension of the writ. However, the fight did not end there by any means. Stephens and his cohorts merely fell back to prepared positions, ranged in depth along the borders of their several sovereign states, and there continued their resistance under the banner of States Rights.

"Georgians, behold your chains!" an Athens newspaper exhorted in an editorial printed alongside the newly passed regulations, which were appropriately framed in mourning borders. "Freemen of a once proud and happy country, contemplate the last act which rivets your bonds and binds you hand and foot, at the mercy of an unlimited military authority." An Alabama editor demanded the names of those congressmen "who, in secret conclave, obsequiously laid the liberties of this country at the feet of the President," so that they could be defeated if they had the gall to stand for reëlection. Henry Foote, having long since warned that he "would call upon the people to rise, sword in hand, to put down the domestic tyrant who thus sought to invade their rights," proceeded to do just that. Nor was this defiance limited to words. Under the leadership of such men, Mississippi and Georgia passed flaming resolutions against the act; Louisiana presently did so, too, and North Carolina soon had a law on its books nullifying the action of the central government. Not even these modifications, crippling as they were to the purpose for which the writ had been suspended, allayed the fears of some that the rights of the states were about to be lost in "consolidation." If such a catastrophe ever came to pass, a Virginian declared, "it would be a kind boon in an overruling Providence to sweep from the earth the soil, along with the people. Better to be a wilderness of waste, than a lasting monument of lost liberty."

A wilderness of waste was what was all too likely to result from this nonrecognition of the fact that the South's whole hope for independence was held up by the bayonets of her soldiers, who in turn required the support of a strong central government if they were to be properly employed — or even, for that matter, clothed and fed — in a years-long conflict so costly in blood and

Confederate vice president Alexander Hamilton Stephens (left) undercut the authority of President Jefferson Davis at every opportunity, citing an obligation to defend the liberties guaranteed by the Confederate Constitution.

money, at the stage it now had reached, that its demands could only be met by the enactment and rigid enforcement of laws which did in fact, as those who opposed them charged, involve the surrender of basic "rights" hitherto reserved to the states and the individual. Yet this was the one sacrifice the "impossiblists," who valued their rights above their chance at national independence, could not make. "Away with the idea of getting independence first, and looking after liberty afterwards," Stephens had said. "Our liberties, once lost, may be lost forever." "Why, sir," a Georgia congressman exclaimed, "this is a war for the Constitution! It is a *constitutional* war."

It was also, and first, a war for survival; but the ultraconservatives, including the fire-eaters who had done so much to bring it on, had been using the weapon of States Rights too long and with too much success, when they were members of the Union, to discard it now that they had seceded. They simply would rather die than drop that cudgel, even when there was no one to use it on but their own people and nothing to strike at except the solidarity that was their one hope for victory over an adversary whose reserves of men and wealth were practically limitless. It was in this inflexibility that the bill came due for having launched a conservative revolution, and apparently it was necessarily so, even though their anomalous devotion to an untimely creed amounted to an irresistible death-wish. But that was precisely their pride. They had inherited it and they would hand it down, inviolate, to the latest generation; or they would pray God "to sweep from the earth the soil, along with the people."

No more than a casual glance at the map sufficed to show the gravity of the military situation they would not relax their civil vigilance to face. Shaded, the Federal gains of the past two years resembled the broad shadow of a bird suspended in flight above the Mississippi Valley, its head hung over Missouri, its tail spread down past New Orleans, and its wings extended from Chesapeake Bay to Texas. What shape the present year would give this shadow was far from clear to those who lived in its penumbra, but they saw clearly enough that the creature who cast it could not be driven back into the land from which it had emerged; at any rate, not to stay there. R. E. Lee, after two expensive attempts to do just that, admitted as much to Davis in early February. "We are not in a condition, and never have been, in my opinion, to invade the enemy's country with a prospect of permanent benefit," he wrote, although he added that he hoped, by means of a show of force in East Tennessee or Virginia, to "alarm and embarrass him to some extent, and thus prevent his undertaking anything of magnitude against us."

Davis agreed that the South was limited by necessity to the strategic defensive. Indeed, that had been his policy from the start, pursued in the belief that Europe would intervene if the struggle could be protracted. The difference now lay in the object of such protraction. Foreign intervention was obviously never going to come, but he still hoped for intervention of another kind. In the North, a presidential election would be held in November, and he hoped for intervention by a majority of the voters, who then would have their chance to end the bloodshed by replacing Lincoln with a man who stood for peace. Peace, no matter whether it was achieved in the North or the South, in the field or at the polls, meant victory on the terms the Confederate leader had announced at the outset, saying, "All we ask is to be let alone." In the light of this possibility, the South's task was to add to the war weariness of the North; which meant, above all, that the enemy was to be allowed no more spirit-lifting triumphs — especially none like Vicksburg or Missionary Ridge, which had set all the church bells ringing beyond the Potomac and the Ohio — and that

> *"We are not in a condition, and never have been,*
> *in my opinion, to invade the enemy's country*
> *with a prospect of permanent benefit."*
>
> — Robert E. Lee

whatever was lost, under pressure of the odds, must not only be minor in value, but must also be paid for in casualties so heavy that the gain would be clearly disproportionate to the cost, particularly in the judgment of those who would be casting their ballots in November.

On the face of it — by contrast, that is, with the two preceding years, each of which had included the added burden of launching an invasion that had failed — this did not appear too difficult a task. In the past calendar year, moreover, while the Federal over-all strength was declining from 918,211 to 860,737 men, that of the Confederates increased from 446,622 to 463,181. This was not only the largest number of men the South had had under arms since the war began; it was also nearly 100,000 more than she had had two years ago, on the eve of her greatest triumphs. However, such encouragement as Davis might have derived from a comparison of these New Year's figures, showing the North-South odds reduced to less than two to one, was short-lived. One month later, Lincoln issued his call for "500,000 more."

That was better than ten times the number Lee had on the Rapidan, covering Richmond, or Johnston had around Dalton, covering Atlanta, and since the loss of either of these cities, in addition to being a strategic disaster for the South, would provide the North with a triumph that would be likely to win Lincoln the election, Davis was faced at once with the problem of how to match

★

this call with one of his own. But the hard truth was that nothing like half that many troops — the number required if the current odds were not to be lengthened intolerably for the savage fighting that would open in the spring — could be raised under the present conscription laws, even though these had been strengthened in December by the passage of legislation that modified exemptions, put an end to the hiring of substitutes, and provided for the replacement of able-bodied men, in noncombatant jobs, with veterans who had been incapacitated by wounds or civilians who previously had been passed over for reasons of health. The bottom of the manpower barrel was not only in sight; it had been scraped practically clean to provide the army with every available male within the conscription age-range of eighteen to forty-five. One possibility, unpleasant to contemplate since it would expose the government more than ever to the charge that it was "robbing the cradle and the grave," would be to extend the range in either or both directions. Another possibility, far more fruitful, was suggested by Pat Cleburne; but it was worse than unpleasant, it was unthinkable.

In early January the Irish-born former Helena lawyer prepared and read to his fellow generals in the Army of Tennessee a paper in which he examined the sinking fortunes of the Confederacy and proposed to deal simultaneously with what he conceived to be the two main problems blocking the path to independence: the manpower shortage, which was growing worse with every victory or defeat, and slavery, which he saw as a millstone the nation could no longer afford to carry in its effort to stay afloat on the sea of war. In brief, Cleburne's proposal was that the South emancipate its Negroes — thus making a virtue of necessity, since in his opinion slavery was doomed anyhow — and enlist them in its armies. This would "change the race from a dreaded weakness to a [source] of strength," he declared, and added: "We can do this more effectually than the North can now do, for we can give the Negro not only his own freedom, but that of his wife and child, and can secure it to him in his old home." Moreover, he said, such an action "would remove forever all selfish taint from our cause and place independence above every question of property. The very magnitude of the sacrifice itself, such as no nation has ever voluntarily made before, would appall our enemies . . . and fill our hearts with a pride and singleness of purpose which would clothe us with new strength in battle."

Recovering presently from the shock into which the foreign-born general's views had thrown them, the corps and division commanders were unanimous in their condemnation of the proposal, which they saw as a threat to everything they held dear. "I will not attempt to describe my feelings on being confronted by a project so startling in its character," one wrote in confidence to a friend. He labeled the paper a "monstrous proposition . . . revolting to Southern sentiment, Southern pride, and Southern honor," and predicted that "if this thing is once openly proposed to the army the total disintegration of that army

★

Realizing the sinking fortunes of the Confederacy, Major General Patrick R. Cleburne proposed a southern emancipation proclamation to increase military manpower and remove the stigma of slavery.

will follow in a fortnight." Advised by Johnston and the others to proceed no further with the matter, Cleburne did not insist that the paper be forwarded, but another general considered it so "incendiary" in character that he took the trouble to get a copy and send it on to Richmond.

There the reaction was much the same, apparently, as the one it had provoked in Dalton. Johnston received, before the month was out, a letter from the Secretary of War, expressing "the earnest conviction of the President that the dissemination or even promulgation of such opinions under the present circumstances of the Confederacy, whether in the army or among the people, can be productive only of discouragement, distraction, and dissension." The army commander was instructed to see to "the suppression, not only of the memorial itself, but likewise of all discussion and controversy respecting or growing out of it." Johnston replied that Cleburne, having observed the manner in which it was received, had already "put away his paper," and that he himself had had "no reason since to suppose that it made any impression." In point of fact, the suppression Richmond called for was so effective that nothing further was heard of the document for more than thirty years, when it finally turned up among the posthumous papers of a staff officer. One possible effect it had, however, and that was on Cleburne himself, or in any case on his career. Although Seddon had assured Johnston that "no doubt or mistrust is for a moment entertained of the patriotic intents of the gallant author of the memorial," and though the Arkansan was considered by many to be the best division commander in either army, South or North, he was never assigned any larger duties than those he had at the time he proposed to emancipate the slaves of the South and enlist them in her struggle for independence.

Davis had not been as shocked by the proposal as Seddon's letter seemed to indicate. For one thing, he agreed with the underlying premise that slavery was doomed, no matter who won or lost the war, and had said as much to his wife. What alarmed him was the reaction, the "distraction and dissension," that would follow the release of what one of its hearers had called "this monstrous proposition." Knowing, as he did, how much more violent than the generals the politicians would be in their denunciation of such views — particularly the large slaveholders among them, such as Howell Cobb, who said flatly: "If slaves will make good soldiers, our whole theory of slavery is wrong" — he foresaw that the result would be calamitous in its effect on the fortunes of the Confederacy, which would be so torn internally by any discussion of the issue that, even though the army could be doubled in size by adoption of the plan, there would be nothing left for that army to defend but discord. Even so, Davis did not completely reject the notion. He kept it — much as Lincoln had kept the Emancipation Proclamation — as an ace in the hole, to be played if all else failed.

Meantime he still was faced with the necessity for matching, at least to some degree, his adversary's call for more additional troops than there were at present in all the southern armies. Left with the alternative of extending conscription, he moved to do so in a message to Congress suggesting 1) that all industrial exemptions be abolished and 2) that the upper and lower age-range limits be raised and reduced, respectively, to fifty and seventeen. The first of these two suggestions kicked up the greater furor. Newspaper editors, who feared (groundlessly, as it turned out) that they would lose their printers if the law was strengthened to this extent, protested that freedom of the press was threatened. For others, the fear was more general. A Virginia congressman, for example, asserted that such legislation would "clothe the President with the powers of an autocrat" and invest him with "prerogatives before which those of Napoleon sink into insignificance," while Foote rose up again in his wrath to declare that "Others may vote to extend this man's power for mischief; I hold in contempt him and his whole tribe of servitors and minions." There were, however, enough of the "tribe" — or, in any case, enough of Foote's colleagues of all persuasions who saw the need for keeping the army up to a strength that would enable it to challenge the blue host that would be advancing with the spring — for the proposed measure to be adopted on February 17, the day Congress adjourned. Word went out at once to the conscription agents of the enlargement of the harvest they would be gleaning. No drawing of lots, no "wheels of fortune," such as were used in the North to select candidates for induction, were required in the South. From this time forward, it was simply the task of the agents to enroll or exempt every white male in the Confederacy between the ages of seventeen and fifty.

Davis's reaction to this granting of his request was mixed. Pleased though he was to have the measure passed, and though he himself had asked for what had been given, he was saddened by the widening of the age-range: not by the raising of the upper limit, which brought it within five years of his own age, but by the reduction of the lower limit, which seemed to him a spending of future hopes. The old and the middle-aged could be spared. The young were another matter. The South would have great need, in the years ahead, of all the talent she could muster — as much, perhaps, if she lost the war, as if she won it — yet there was no telling how much of that talent, still undeveloped at seventeen, would be destroyed and left behind, packed into shallow burial trenches on the fields of battles still unfought. It grieved him that the mill of war, as he remarked, was about to "grind the seed corn of the nation."

While the young and the old were thus being gathered in camps of instruction, where they would be converted into material fit for use in chinking what he once had called "our wall of living breasts," Davis gave his attention to strengthening and replacing the men who would lead them. The appointment in early January of George Davis of North Carolina to succeed Attorney General Watts, who had left Richmond the month before to be inaugurated as governor of Alabama, marked the first change in the Cabinet since Seddon took over the War Department, more than a year ago. Little attention was paid to this, for the post entailed few duties; but the same could not be said of two changes that followed, for they were military, and anything that involved the army was always of consuming interest. Before adjourning, Congress had authorized the President to appoint a sixth full general, thus to allow a freer hand to the commander of the Transmississippi, cut off as he was from either the direction or assistance of the central government. Davis's prompt award of the promotion to Kirby Smith, for whom of course it had been intended, was applauded by everyone, in or out of the army, except Longstreet, whose name headed the list of lieutenant generals, on which Smith's had stood second. "A soldier's honor is his all," Old Peter afterwards protested, "and of that they would rob him and degrade him in the eyes of his troops." Piqued at having thus been overleaped — and unhappy as he was anyhow, because of his late repulse at Knoxville and the disaffection that had spread through his corps in its mountainous camps around Greeneville, seventy miles to the east — his first reaction was that "the occasion seemed to demand resignation." But on second thought he decided that this "would have been unsoldierly conduct. Dispassionate judgment suggested, as the proper rounding of the soldier's life, to stay and go down with faithful comrades of long and arduous service."

Painful though the burning was in Longstreet's ample bosom, it was no more than a pinpoint gleam compared to the fires of resentment lighted by the announcement, a few days later, of the second military change. On February 22, the second anniversary of his inauguration as head of the permanent government, Davis summoned Lee to the capital for another conference. There were matters of strategy to be discussed, and something else as well. The Virginian's former post as advisor to the Commander in Chief had been vacant for more than twenty months; now Davis proposed to name Bragg as his successor. This was certain to surprise and dismay a great many people who saw the North Carolinian as the author of most of their present woes, but Davis believed that Bragg's undeniable shortcomings as a field commander — particularly his tendency to convert drawn battles into defeats by retreating, and victories into stalemates by failing to pursue — were not disqualifications for service in an advisory capacity; whereas his equally undeniable virtues, as an administrator and a strategist — his northward march into Kentucky, for example, undertaken on his own initiative at a time of deepest gloom, had reversed the whole course of the war in the western theater, and he had also proved himself (all too often, some would say) a master in the art of conducting tactical withdrawals — would be of great value to the country. Lee agreed, and the appointment was announced two days later, on February 24: "General Braxton Bragg is assigned to duty at the seat of government, and, under the direction of the President, is charged with the conduct of the military operations in the armies of the Confederacy."

Surprise and dismay, private and public, were indeed the reactions to the terrible-tempered general's elevation, coming as it did only one day short of three months since his rout at Missionary Ridge. "No doubt Bragg can give the President valuable counsel," a War Department diarist observed, but in his opinion Davis — whom he described as being "naturally a little oppugnant" — derived "a secret satisfaction in triumphing thus over popular sentiment, which just at this time is much averse to General Bragg." The sharpest attacks, as might have been expected, were launched by the editors of the Richmond *Whig* and the *Examiner*. Both employed irony in their comments, ignoring the advisory nature of Bragg's assignment by pretending to believe that Davis had given his pet general direct command over Lee and Johnston. "When a man fails in an inferior position," the *Whig* declared, "it is natural and charitable to conclude that the failure is due to the inadequacy of the task to his capabilities, and wise to give him a larger sphere for the proper exertion of his abilities." Pollard of the *Examiner* struck with a heavier hand, though his pen was no less sharp. "The judicious and opportune appointment of General Bragg to the post of commander-in-chief of the Confederate armies will be appreciated," he noted wryly, "as an illustration of that strong common sense which forms the basis of the President's character." He managed to sustain this tone for half a column, then dropped it in midsentence: "This happy announcement should enliven the confidence and enthusiasm reviving among the people like a bucket of water poured on a newly kindled grate."

★

Davis went his way, as he had done from the beginning. "If we succeed we shall hear nothing of these malcontents," he had told his wife three years ago in Montgomery. "If we do not, then I shall be held accountable by friends as well as foes. I will do my best." That was as much his guiding principle now as ever. He believed that Bragg would serve him and the country well in this new assignment, and so far as he was concerned the decision as to whether to use him ended there. "Opposition in any form can only disturb me inasmuch as it may endanger the public welfare," he had said. For all his aristocratic bearing and his apparent indifference to the barbs flung at him by men like Foote and Pollard, which gave rise to the persistent myth that he was deficient in feeling, he trusted the people far more than he did the politicians and journalists who catered to their weaknesses and fears, and he knew only too well the hardness of their lot in this season of lengthening death lists and spiraling inflation. Ten Confederate dollars would buy a yard of calico or a pound of coffee; bacon was $3.50 a pound, butter $4; eggs were $2 a dozen, chickens $6 a pair. Such prices made for meager living, particularly for city dwellers who had no vegetable gardens to tend or harvest. But even these were fortunate, so far at least as food was concerned, in comparison with the soldiers. The daily ration in the Army of Northern Virginia this winter was four ounces of bacon or salt pork and one pint of unbolted cornmeal, and though a private was free to scrounge what he could in his off hours, including wild onions and dandelion greens, his pay of $11 a month would not go far toward the purchase of supplements, even when they were available, which was seldom.

*This Confederate $500 bill, issued in
February 1863, commemorates the fallen
General Thomas "Stonewall" Jackson.*

Still, there were those who seemed to make out well enough from time to time: as a hungry infantryman, out on a greens hunt, discovered one day when he came upon a group of commissary officers enjoying an al fresco luncheon in the shade of a clump of trees. He approached the fence surrounding the grove, put his head through the palings, and gazed admiringly at the spread of food. "I say, misters," he called to the diners at last, "did any of you ever hearn tell of the battle of Chance'lorsville?"

This irrepressibility, which sustained him in adversity, this overriding sense of the ridiculous, uncramped even by the pangs of hunger, was as much a part of what made the Confederate soldier "terrible in battle" as was the high-throated yell he gave when he went into a charge or the derisive glee with which he tended to receive one, anticipating a yield of well-shod corpses. Davis counted heavily on this spirit to insure the survival of the armies and the nation through the harder times he knew would begin when the present "mud truce" ended. He was too much a military realist not to take into account the lengthening odds, but he included the imponderables in his calculations. To have done otherwise would have been to admit defeat before it came; which was not at all his way. "I cultivate hope and patience," he said, "and trust to the blunders of our enemy and the gallantry of our troops for ultimate success."

I n the North, as spring drew nearer and some perspective was afforded for a backward look at the season approaching its end, there was the feeling that such minor reverses as Olustee and Okolona, disappointing though they had been at the time, were no true detractions from the significant victories scored at the outset at Rappahannock Bridge and Chattanooga. These were the pattern-setters, the more valid indications of what was to come when winter relaxed its grip and large-scale fighting was resumed. Along with this, there was also the growing belief that the nation had found in Lincoln, despite his occasional military errors, the leader it needed to see it through what remained of its fiery trial. "The President is a man of convictions," *Harper's Weekly* had declared more than a year ago, combining these two impressions. "He has certain profound persuasions and a very clear purpose. He knows what the war sprang from, and upon what ground a permanent peace can be reared. He is cautious, cool, judicial. [While] he knows that great revolutions do not go backward, he is aware that when certain great steps in their prosecution are once taken, there will be loud outcries and apprehension. But the ninth wave touches the point to which the whole sea will presently rise, although the next wave, and the next, should seem to show a falling off."

★

What *Harper's* had had in mind at the time was the Emancipation Proclamation, but people rereading this now could see that Missionary Ridge had been just such a ninth wave, lapping far up the military shingle, and though "the next wave, and the next," had shown a falling off, the tide would soon be at the full. Or anyhow they could believe they saw this, and they reacted accordingly. During the current interim of comparative inaction, the home-front war had taken on what would be known in the following decade as a Chautauqua aspect, a revival of the waning lyceum movement, which combined the qualities of the camp meeting and the county fair, yet added a sophistication those old-time activities had lacked. They assembled in churches, halls, and theaters to enjoy in mass the heady atmosphere of pending victory. Primarily, such gatherings were militant in tone — meaning abolitionist, for the antislavery element had always been the militant wing of the party now in power — with the result that those who attended could feel that they were being strengthened and uplifted at the same time they were being entertained.

There was, for example, the Hutchinson family: singers who could electrify an audience with their rendition of Whittier's "Hymn, of Liberty," sung to the tune of Luther's *Ein' feste Burg ist unser Gott*. The thought might be muddled, the rhymes atrocious, but the sweetness of the singers' voice and the fervor of their delivery gave the words a power that swept the hearers along as part of the broad surge toward that same freedom for which blue-clad soldiers were giving their lives, beyond the roll of the horizon:

> *What gives the wheat-field blades of steel?*
>
> *What points the rebel cannon?*
>
> *What sets the roaring rabble's heel*
>
> *On the old star-spangled pennon?*
>
> *What breaks the oath*
>
> *Of the men o' the South?*
>
> *What whets the knife*
>
> *For the Union's life?*
>
> *Hark to the answer: Slavery!*

Or there was the Boston lecturer Wendell Phillips, who assured a New York audience of its moral superiority over a foe whose only role in life was to block the march of progress. He pictured the young man of the South, "melted in sensuality, whose face was never lighted up by a purpose since his

An ardent abolitionist, Wendell Phillips often cursed the Constitution for permitting slavery, and he refused to support it by running for public office — or even voting.

mother looked into his cradle," and declared that for such men "War is gain. They go out of it, and they sink down." Whipped, they would return "to bar-rooms, to corner groceries, to chopping straw and calling it politics. [Laughter.] You might think they would go back to their professions. They never had any. You might think they would go back to the mechanic arts. They don't know how to open a jackknife. [Great merriment.] There is nowhere for them to go, unless we send them half a million of emancipated blacks to teach them how to plant cotton." His solution to the problem of how to keep the beaten South from relapsing "into a state of society more cruel than war — whose characteris-tics are private assassination, burning, stabbing, shooting, poisoning" — lifted the North's grim efforts to the height of a crusade: "We have not only an army to conquer. We have a state of mind to annihilate."

Phillips could always fill a hall, but the star attraction this season, all agreed, was the girl orator Anna E. Dickinson, who had begun her career on the eve of her twentieth birthday, when she lost her job at the mint in her native Philadelphia for accusing McClellan of treason at Ball's Bluff. Since then, she had come far, until now she was hailed alternately as the Joan of Arc and the Portia of the Union. Whether she spoke at the Academy of Music in her home city, at New York's Cooper Union, or at the Music Hall in Boston, the

★

house was certain to be packed with those who came to marvel at the contrast between her virginal appearance — "her features well chiseled, her forehead and upper lip of the Greek proportion, her nostrils thin" — and the "torrent of burning, scathing, lightning eloquence," which she released in what the same reviewer called "wonderfully lengthened sentences uttered without break or pause." Hearing Anna was a dramatic experience not easily forgotten, though what you brought away with you was not so much a remembrance of what she had said as it was of the manner in which she had said it: which was how she affected Henry James, apparently, when he came to portray her, more than twenty years later, as Verena Tarrant. Her hatred of Southerners, especially Jefferson Davis, whom she compared to a hyena, was not so all-consuming that none was left for northern Democrats, who were without exception traitors to the cause of human freedom — as, indeed, were all who were not of the most radical persuasion, including such Republicans as Seward, "the Fox of the White House." She loved applause; it thrilled her, and her style became more forward as her listeners responded; so that her addresses were in a sense a form of intercourse, an exchange of emotions, back and forth across the footlights.

Quite different, but curious too in her effect on those who came to hear and see her, was another platform artist, the former slave Sojourner Truth. Tall and gaunt, utterly black, and close to eighty years of age, she made her appearances in a voluminous, floor-length, long-sleeved dress, a crocheted shawl, and the calico turban or headrag that was practically a badge of office for house servants in the South, particularly children's nurses; which was what she had been, before she won her freedom and came North. Battle Creek was now her home, and she journeyed not only through Michigan, but also through Illinois and Indiana and Ohio, including the Copperhead regions of those states, to plead for the extension of freedom to all her race, north as well as south of the Proclamation line. She spoke in a deep, musical voice, with natural grace and simple dignity, and vended as a side line, to help cover her travel expenses, photographs of herself in her speaking costume; "selling the shadow to sustain the substance," she explained. Her most valued possession, despite her illiteracy, was an autograph book containing the signatures of famous men and women she encountered along her way, one of whom would presently be the Great Emancipator himself. "For Aunty Sojourner Truth, A. Lincoln," he wrote, and she gave him one of her photographs, remarking that she sold them for her livelihood, "but this one is for you, without money and without price." She was much admired, though for the most part as an exotic, and was generally welcome wherever she went, although not always. Once in an Indiana town, for instance, when she was introduced to deliver an antislavery address to a large audience, a local Copperhead rose to repeat the rumor that she was a man, disguised in women's clothes, and to suggest that she permit a committee of ladies to examine her in private. She answered the challenge, then and there, by unfastening her dress and showing the crowd her shrunken, hound's-ear breasts. These had fed many black children, she said, but still more white children had nursed at them. By now the Copperheads — who had come to watch her, or his, exposure as a fraud — were filing out of the auditorium, a look of disgust on their faces, and Sojourner Truth jiggled her breasts at one of them, inquiring after him in her low contralto: "You want to suck?"

Wendell Phillips, Anna Dickinson, Sojourner Truth were only three among the many who were riding the wave of confidence that the worst was over, that the war could have but one ending now, and that it would come as soon as the South could be made to see what already was apparent in the North. Moreover, there had come with this belief a lessening of discord, not only among the people, but also in the conduct of affairs in Washington. "Never since I have been in public life has there been so little excitement in Congress," Sumner wrote on New Year's Day to a friend in England. "The way seems, at last, open. Nobody doubts the result. The assurance of the future gives calmness." This did not mean that the legislators were willing to take chances. Knowing as they did that the public's blame for any failure would be in ratio to the height of its expectations, they were in fact less willing to take chances than they had been at any time before.

Sojourner Truth was a popular speaker at abolitionist rallies. Her plain talk about the evils of slavery moved many audiences, and her wit silenced those who dared to challenge her.

★

It was for this reason that the bill to revive the grade of lieutenant general had itself been revived: to reduce the likelihood of military blunders at the top. "Give us, Sir, a live general!" a Michigan senator exclaimed in the course of the debate. He meant by this a man who would follow a straight path to victory, "and not let us be dragging along under influences such as have presided over the Army of the Potomac for these last many tedious and weary months; an army oscillating alternately between the Rappahannock and the Potomac, defeated today and hardly successful tomorrow, with its commanders changed almost as frequently as the moon changes its face. Sir, for one I am tired of this, and I tell [the] senators here that the country is getting weary of it."

Some proponents were in favor of naming Grant specifically in the bill, while others believed that this would be setting a dangerous precedent. Besides, Fessenden of Maine rose to ask, to whom could the promotion go if not to Grant? and then went on to point out that the honor would be greater if no name was mentioned, since to do so would be to imply that there had been a choice: "When the President says to us, as he will say unquestionably, 'I consider that General Ulysses S. Grant is the man of all others, from his great services, to be placed in this exalted position,' and when we, as we shall unquestionably, unanimously say 'Ay' to that and confirm him, have we not given him a position such as any man living or who ever lived might well be proud of, without putting his name in our bill originally and thus saying to the President, 'Sir, we cannot trust you to act on this matter unless we hint to you that we want such a man appointed'?"

Lengthy and thorough the debate was, but there was never much doubt as to the outcome. Introduced on the first day of February, the measure was passed on the last, and the procedure Fessenden had outlined followed swiftly. Receiving the bill on March 1, Lincoln promptly signed it and named Grant for the honor next day. The Senate confirmed the appointment without delay, and on March 3 the general was ordered by telegraph to report at once to Washington, where he would receive his commission directly from the President.

Lincoln had been disappointed too often, over the course of the past three years, for him to allow his hopes to soar too high. He remembered McDowell and McClellan. He remembered Burnside and Hooker. Above all, he remembered Pope, who had also come East with western laurels on his brow. And there at hand, in case memory failed, was Halleck; Old Brains, too, had arrived from that direction, supposedly with a victory formula in his knapsack, and had wound up "a first-rate clerk." Still, after making all proper discounts, it seemed likely to Lincoln that now at last, in this general who had captured two rebel armies and routed a third, he had found the killer-arithmetician he had been seeking from the start.

★　★　★

Federal soldiers mount guard on the ramparts of Nashville's Fort Negley in this photograph of the fort and terrain made for Sherman's engineers in early 1864.

Grant Summoned to Washington

1864 ★ ★ ★ ★ ★ **R**eturning to Vicksburg on the last day of February, Sherman took no time out to recuperate from the rigors of the Meridian campaign, for he found there a week-old dispatch from Grant instructing him to coöperate with Banks in order to assure the success of the expedition up the Teche and the Red, which the Massachusetts general and Halleck had designed to accomplish the return of West Louisiana and East Texas to the Union, along with an estimated half million bales of hoarded cotton. Sherman himself was to rejoin Grant at Chattanooga in time to open the spring drive on Atlanta; he would therefore not participate in the Louisiana-Texas venture, save for making a short-term loan of some 10,000 troops to strengthen it; but he decided to confer in person with Banks, before he himself went back to Tennessee, on the logistical details of getting the reinforcements to him somewhere up the Red. Accordingly, he left Vicksburg that same day aboard the fast packet *Diana,* and arrived in New Orleans two days later, on March 2.

He found Banks in high spirits: not only because of the military outlook, which was considered excellent — Franklin had recovered from his early November repulse at Grand Coteau and had three divisions massed at Opelousas, ready to advance — but also because of political developments in

★

accordance with Lincoln's reconstruction policy, whereby a Union-loyal candi-date, one Michael Hahn, a native of Bavaria, had been elected governor of Louisiana by the necessary ten percent of the voters on February 22 and was to be inaugurated at New Orleans on March 5. Sherman's logistical problems were settled within two days, the arrangement being that the Vicksburg reinforce-ments would join Franklin at Alexandria on March 17 for the farther ascent of the Red, but Banks urged his visitor to stay over another two days for Hahn's inauguration, which he assured him would be well worth the delay. A chorus of one thousand voices, accompanied by all the bands of the army, would perform the "Anvil Chorus" in Lafayette Square, while church bells rang and cannon were fired in unison by electrical devices.

Sherman declined the invitation. He had already gone on record as opposing such political procedures, and what was more, he said later, "I regarded all such ceremonies as out of place at a time when it seemed to me every hour and every minute were due to the war." His mind on destruction, not reconstruction, he reboarded the *Diana,* and three days later, on March 6, was back in Vicksburg, to which by now the destroyers of Meridian had returned, well rested from their week-long stay in Canton and the additional spoliation they had accomplished at that place.

Remaining in Vicksburg only long enough to pass on to McPherson the details of the arrangement he had made for reinforcing Banks at Alexandria on St Patrick's Day, Sherman set off upriver again the following morning, impatient to rejoin the troops he had left poised near Chattanooga, waiting alongside those under Thomas and Hooker for Grant to give the nod that would start them slogging southward, over or around Joe Johnston, into and through the heart of Georgia. "Prepare them for my coming," he had told his adjutant, in reference to the hapless civilians in his path, and now at last he was on his way. On the second day out, however, the *Diana* was hailed by a southbound packet which, to the Ohioan's surprise, turned out to have one of Grant's staff captains aboard, charged with the delivery of a highly personal letter his chief had written four days ago, on March 4, at Nashville.

"Dear Sherman," it read: "The bill reviving the grade of lieutenant general in the army has become a law, and my name has been sent to the Senate for the place. I now receive orders to report to Washington immediately, in per-son, which indicates either a confirmation or a likelihood of confirmation. I start in the morning to comply with the order, but I shall say very distinctly on my arrival there that I shall accept no appointment which will require me to make that city my headquarters. This, however, is not what I started out to write about. . . . What I want is to express my thanks to you and McPherson as the men to whom, above all others, I feel indebted for whatever I have had of success. How far your advice and suggestions have been of assistance, you know.

★

This late 1863 portrait shows Major General Ulysses S. Grant shortly before he gained a third star, becoming the first officer since George Washington to hold the full grade of lieutenant general in the U.S. Army.

How far your execution of whatever has been given you to do entitles you to the reward I am receiving, you cannot know as well as I do. I feel all the gratitude this letter would express, giving it the most flattering construction. The word *you* I use in the plural, intending it for McPherson also," the letter concluded. "I should write to him, and will some day, but starting in the morning I do not know that I will find time just now. Your friend, U. S. Grant."

Sherman vibrated with three conflicting reactions as he read the first three sentences Grant had written: first, delight that his friend was about to be so honored: second, alarm that he had been summoned to the fleshpots of the capital: third, relief that he did not intend to stay there. However, as the boat continued to push its way slowly upriver against the booming current, the third emotion gave way in turn to the second, which came back even stronger than at first. The fact was, though he idolized his friend and superior, he had never really trusted his judgment in matters concerning his career, and though he admired his simplicity of character, seeing it in the quality that perhaps had contributed most to his success, he was forever supposing that it would get him in trouble, especially if he fell into the hands of wily men who would know how to use him for their sordid ends. "Your reputation as a general is now far above that of any man living, and partisans will maneuver for your influence," he had warned him in a letter written during the Christmas visit to Ohio, at a time when the Grant-for-President drums were beginning to rumble. He counseled him earnestly to "Preserve a plain military character and let others maneuver as they will. You will beat them not only in fame, but in doing good in the closing scenes of this war, when somebody must heal and mend up the breaches."

Nowhere were the wily more in evidence than in Washington, and the more he thought about it, the more he was convinced that "Grant would not stand the intrigues of the politicians a week," even though he went there with no intention of remaining any longer than it took to get a third star tacked on each shoulder of his weathered blouse. What was more, Sherman had a mystical feeling about the Mississippi River, which he called "the great artery" of America. "I want to live out here and die here also," he wrote to another friend

---

"For God's sake and your country's sake,
come out of Washington!"

— William T. Sherman

---

this week, as the *Diana* chugged upstream, "and I don't care if my grave be like De Soto's in its muddy waters." He seemed to fear that if Grant wandered far from the banks of the big river, his reaction would be like that of Antaeus when he lost contact with the earth.

Accordingly, after two days of fretting and fuming, as the boat drew near Memphis on March 10 he dashed off an answer to Grant's "more than kind and characteristic letter," thanking him in McPherson's name and his own, but protesting: "You do yourself injustice and us too much honor in assigning us so large a share of the merits which have led to your high advancement. . . . At Belmont you manifested your traits, neither of us being near. At Donelson also you illustrated your character; I was not near, and General McPherson [was] in too subordinate a capacity to influence you. Until you had won Donelson, I confess I was almost cowed by the terrible array of anarchical elements that presented themselves at every point; but that victory admitted the ray of light which I have followed ever since. . . . The chief characteristic in your nature is the simple faith in success you have always manifested, which I can liken to nothing else than the faith a Christian has in his Saviour. This faith gave you victory at Shiloh and Vicksburg. Also, when you have completed your best preparations, you go into battle without hesitation, as at Chattanooga; no doubts, no reserve; and I tell you that it was this that made us act with confidence. I knew wherever I was that you thought of me, and if I got in a tight place you would come — if alive. My only points of doubt were as to your knowledge of grand strategy and of books of science and history, but I confess your commonsense seems to have supplied all this."

Having disposed thus of the disclaimers and the amenities, the volatile redhead passed at once to the main burden of his letter. If Grant stayed East, Sherman almost certainly would be given full charge of the West, and yet, although personally he wanted this above all possible assignments, he was unwilling to secure it at the cost of his friend's ruin, which was what he believed would result from any such arrangement. "Do not stay in Washington," he urged him. "Halleck is better qualified than you are to stand the buffets of intrigue and policy. Come out West; take to yourself the whole Mississippi Valley. Let us make it dead sure, and I tell you the Atlantic slope and Pacific shores will follow its destiny as sure as the limbs of a tree live or die with the main trunk. We have done much; still much remains. . . . For God's sake and your country's sake, come out of Washington! I foretold to General Halleck, before he left Corinth, the inevitable result to him, and I now exhort you to come out West. Here lies the seat of the coming empire, and from the West, when our task is done, we will make short work of Charleston and Richmond and the impoverished coast of the Atlantic."

Within a week he found his warning had been too late. Arriving in Memphis next day he received on March 14 a message from Grant arranging a meeting in Nashville three days later. If Sherman took this as evidence that his chief did not intend to make his headquarters in the East, he soon learned better. In Nashville on the appointed date, invested with the rank of lieutenant general and command of all the armies of the Union, Grant informed him that the Virginia situation required personal attention; he would be returning there to stay, and Sherman would have full charge of the West. However, what with the press of visiting dignitaries, all anxious for a look at a man with three stars on each shoulder, there was so little time for a strategy conference that it was decided the two generals would travel together as far as Cincinnati on Grant's return trip east. That way, it was thought, they could talk on the cars; but the wheels made such a clatter, they finally gave up trying to shout above the racket and fell silent. In Cincinnati they checked into the Burnet House, and there at last, in a private room with a sentry at the door, they spread their maps and got to work.

"Yonder began the campaign," Sherman was to say a quarter century later, standing before the hotel on the occasion of a visit to the Ohio city. "He was to go for Lee and I was to go for Joe Johnston. That was his plan."

★ ★ ★

★

Epilogue

⋆ ⋆ ⋆ In early 1864 nothing much seemed to be going right for either side, although each was searching for the right combinations to break the recent apparent stalemate. Union general George Meade finally took the initiative against the Confederates, but a combination of slowness and bad weather allowed Robert E. Lee to maneuver into a position at Mine Run so unassailable that even the Federals realized an attack would be suicidal. The Army of the Potomac and the Army of Northern Virginia alike went into winter camp and rested, watched, and waited. The Confederacy had launched the *H. L. Hunley,* an experimental vessel aimed at breaking the Union blockade. The boat was the first submarine to successfully sink an enemy vessel, the venerable *Housatonic,* but a one-time success was all she got — the *Hunley,* too, was sunk in the encounter.

Lincoln, facing reëlection in the coming fall, moved on several fronts to solidify his position. He had proposed an offer of amnesty — if ten percent of the people of a southern state would sign a loyalty oath, the state could reënter the Union — which outraged northern radical Republicans and Southerners alike. Yet two invasions of rebel territory derived from the vain hope that Southerners would accept that amnesty. Leaving Hilton Head, South Carolina, with a large supply of amnesty oath forms, the first attempt was undertaken to invade central Florida. But horrendous terrain, poor logistics, a lack of local support, and state militiamen who put up a fight at Olustee sent the Federals scurrying back north. The second was a full-scale, two-pronged cavalry raid on Richmond. The intent of the raid, in addition to disrupting the southern capital and freeing northern prisoners held there, was to distribute amnesty proclamations within the enemy's lines. Judson Kilpatrick's prong hit greater-than-expected resistance in the outer defenses of Richmond and was forced to withdraw. Ulric Dahlgren's prong, approaching the city from the south and west, could find no ford on the swollen James River and, also meeting stiff resistance, withdrew as well. But Dahlgren's men were followed and entrapped and Dahlgren himself killed. Papers found on his body claimed the raid aimed to burn Richmond and kill Jefferson Davis and thereby created a firestorm of denials and recriminations in both the Union and the Confederacy.

In the west, in an attempt to strengthen the Federal hold on Vicksburg, William T. Sherman moved west to destroy Confederate rail lines and resources in central Mississippi. William Sooy Smith's cavalry was to move south from Memphis, destroying what it could on the way, to join Sherman at Meridian. Smith's force was routed far short of the rendezvous by rebel cavalry under Forrest. Sherman had to be content with burning Meridian and withdrawing to Canton and then Vicksburg.

In the face of the seesawing course of the war, both Presidents Davis and Lincoln faced growing opposition at home. Davis implemented several changes and policies that further damaged southern morale and the national unity he had hoped they would improve. Having replaced Bragg with Joseph E. Johnston in the west, he summoned the widely vilified Bragg to Richmond as his military adviser, then pushed through Congress a suspension of habeas corpus, an extension of the draft age from seventeen to fifty, a reduction in the number and types of exemptions, and increased inforcement of conscription. Opposition was tremendous, even from his own vice president, Alexander Stephens, for these regulations contravened the very reason for secession from the Union — the subordination of the rights of individual states to a central government. Once again Salmon Chase, Lincoln's secretary of the Treasury, was at the center of a cabal hoping to deny the president a second term. Once again Lincoln entrapped Chase in his own tangled political web and once again refused his offer of resignation. Lincoln worked with Congress to revive the rank of lieutenant general and offered the position to Grant. This decision was to alter the course of the war. While ongoing campaigns in the west — notably Banks' attempt to expand and consolidate the Federal hold on Louisiana and Texas along the Red River — would follow the well-established patterns of virtually every campaign since First Manassas, as Grant himself put it, the Federal armies had "acted independently and without concert, like a balky team, no two ever pulling together." That was about to change. Under Lieutenant General Ulysses S. Grant's unified command of all of the Union armies, such fragmentation would virtually disappear. From now on, the Federal armies would work in concert. They would be guided by the dual principles of the highest possible concentration of force and continuous actions against the enemy's armed forces and resources until, by attrition, if in no other way, unconditional surrender of the rebels would be achieved.

★   ★   ★

A
CIVIL
WAR
ALBUM

The American Civil War was the first major event to be heavily documented in photographs. By the time the conflict broke out, the craft was barely twenty years old — the first viable photographic process had been introduced to the world in 1839. Those early images were unique, unreproducible mirror reflections captured on small emulsified metal plates. In America, portrait studios sprang up across the country as photographers practiced the new art. But the process was involved and the exposures were long — in the early days it could take ten seconds or more to capture an image. Seated subjects moved less than standing ones. Standing ones often were aided with neck braces, or leaned on tables, canes, and other props to freeze the pose. By the 1850s great advances had been made, and more sensitive emulsions required shorter exposure times — though several seconds still might be required — and the invention of glass plate negatives allowed for inexpensive paper prints. The new processes began to replace the old, and photographers began to leave their studios more frequently to photograph outdoors.

When a photographer took to the field, he often did so with one or two specially designed wagons for carrying equipment and chemicals. Those wagons also served as a darkroom like the one at left. To take a picture, the camera had to be set up on a sturdy tripod, and the image composed. Then, in the wagon, a glass plate was coated with chemicals and enclosed in a lightproof case. The plate was then inserted into the camera, the protective case removed, the lens uncovered to expose the plate to light, the case re-

A Brady photographer (inset, center) was photographed as he prepared to take the image (below) of Federal dead awaiting burial.

turned, and the plate rushed to the wagon by the photographer so the negative could be developed — all in the ten to fifteen minutes before the emulsion dried. Given the complicated procedure and long exposures, it is hardly surprising that there are no action-filled photos of the conflict. Photographers, looking for a more satisfying effect, staged scenes, arranging their subjects to give the feel of informality and action, but the subjects still had to be steadied — individuals held on to swords, rifles, trees, tent poles, wagons, and even comrades — to remain still for the lens. A careful eye can discern a blurred hand, the ghostly impression of a horse that skittered, or the mere wisp of a flag stirred by a breeze.

There are far fewer field and camp photos of Confederates than of Federals. While early in the war there were active southern photographers — men like George S. Cook, who photographed around Charleston, South

Carolina, and J. D. Edwards, covering Bragg's early attacks on Fort Pickens near Pensacola, Florida — the Union blockade of rebel ports greatly reduced the supplies of photographic chemicals and equipment. Therefore, most practicing southern photographers chose to remain in their portrait studios, where they were more or less assured an income, for there were no great outlets for images in the seceding states, as there were in the North.

The South had no Mathew Brady, whose name became virtually synonymous with Civil War photography. From modest beginnings in 1845, with a studio in New York City that took, and a gallery that showed, portraits of leading citizens, Brady expanded his operation, eventually opening another studio and gallery in Washington, D.C. As the war went on, and Brady's already poor vision became worse, he took fewer and fewer images himself but organized one of the biggest and best corps of photographers to take images for him. He collected, archived, displayed, and sold those images. His often cavalier treatment of photographers, his willingness to appropriate images not properly his, and his shoddy accounting practices led Brady into bankruptcy in 1867.

Among the best-known Civil War period photographers were men like Alexander Gardner, George Barnard, Timothy O'Sullivan, and Andrew J. Russell, to name but a few. Gardner and his employer Brady had a falling-out in 1863, and Gardner became the official photographer for the Army Secret Service and then opened a gallery with his own stable of photographers. George Barnard initially worked for Brady too. He later joined Gardner and then served as the official Union photographer in the western theater. After the war, O'Sullivan, another Brady employee, worked as a survey photographer in the far west and later photographed explorations in Panama. A. J. Russell had few if any dealings with Brady. Russell was commissioned a captain in the U.S. Army and served as a photographer for the Construction Corps, documenting its activities as well as making images of other operations and scenes in the Washington, D.C., area. The photographs produced by these men, and hundreds more like them, give us unique and penetrating views of one of the seminal events in American history.

Mathew Brady was the North's best-known photographer and purveyor of images during the Civil War.

The Ones They Loved So Dear

Beginning with the first call to arms in 1861, thousands of Union and Confederate soldiers and their loved ones went to the local photographer's studio. Recent technological advances — primarily a photographic process that yielded inexpensive paper prints — had made it possible for ordinary Americans to have their portraits taken and to get multiple copies. Soldiers, like the Federal lieutenant at left, were eager to pose, usually in uniform, with their children and parents, wives or sweethearts, and brothers and sisters. The soldiers, whether new recruits or veterans, sensed that the war would be the climactic event in their lives, and they meant to leave a record of their participation. While the sitters often appear rigid and strained because of the difficulty of holding still during the long exposures necessary for formal portraits, these images were cherished comfort, whether left at home or carried off to war — reminders of the dear ones who went away or stayed behind. So popular were wartime portraits that poet and essayist Dr. Oliver Wendell Holmes, Sr. called them "the social currency, the sentimental greenbacks of civilization."

An unidentified Confederate captain holds his son (right); the wife of a Federal sergeant sits on his lap (below, left); and a Confederate colonel and his wife hold hands (below, right).

Sisters sit arm in arm with their Confederate brother (below), and a New York corporal (above, right) and a private of the 95th Pennsylvania Zouaves (above, left) pose with their wives.

As all four of them stare intently at the camera, a Union soldier and his younger brother stand stiffly behind their two sisters.

Cloaked and bonneted, Mrs. George K. Brady stands with her hand on her husband's shoulder. He was a lieutenant in the 14th United States Infantry.

The daughter of Private John Q. Pope (left) of the 1st Massachusetts Heavy Artillery clings to her father, and Private Henry Dikeman, 53d New York Zouaves (below, left), sits with his parents and a younger brother, also in uniform.

Texas private John Pickle (left) and Massachusetts sergeant Henry H. Waugh (above) pose with their wives. Below, a Union corporal sits with his family.

Dressed in civilian clothes, a young man stands behind his uniformed Virginia brother and their sister.

Dr. Jonas W. Lyman, photographed with his daughter Libbie, joined the 203d Pennsylvania as a lieutenant colonel in 1864. He was shot through the heart in an assault on Fort Fisher in January of the following year.

Passing Time Away

Battle-scarred veteran of the 20th Massachusetts and later Supreme Court justice Oliver Wendell Holmes, Jr. once commented that "war was an organized bore." When not actively engaged in the terrible business of war, or the endless rounds of drill and fatigue duty, the typical Johnny Reb or Billy Yank spent a great deal of time fighting boredom. Often photographers were present to record the resulting pastimes — card and baseball games, letter writing, fishing *(left)*, religious services, and horseplay, among others. Cumbersome technology denied the picture makers candid shots, so they staged the scenes. While posed and carefully choreographed, their images reveal much of soldier life in camp beyond the obvious activities portrayed. Visible are the tools and techniques of cooking, preparing firewood, and other domestic chores. Living quarters are canvas tents with the sides rolled up to reveal their contents, or sturdy log huts, chinked tight against wintry blasts. Coats off, sleeves rolled up, blouses partially unbuttoned, and nonregulation headgear prove that camp garb was often rather relaxed. Even the pleasures of personal grooming and hygiene are portrayed.

★

Tent flaps raised to let in the breeze, Lieutenant Colonel Samuel W. Owen of the 3d Pennsylvania Cavalry dozes through a hot afternoon in July 1862. The liquor bottle on his cot was probably placed there by a prankster, since as an officer he probably would have carried a flask and a telescoping cup like the ones shown below.

Federal soldiers stand by while a comrade receives a haircut from an amateur barber. After long campaigns, the men looked forward to such amenities; one Confederate recalled that "the luxury of a shave completed the restoration of the man to decency."

Four officers of the 114th Pennsylvania Infantry enjoy a quiet smoke and bottles of wine delivered by servants as they play a hand of cards. Manufactured by a London firm, the cards below sport southern flags and the Great Seal of the Confederacy. Run through the Federal naval blockade, such imports were beyond the reach of the enlisted men, who made do with cheaper or homemade versions.

Federal soldiers take a refreshing swim in Virginia's North Anna River during a brief lull between battles of the Wilderness campaign of 1864. For many of these men, it was the first opportunity to bathe in several weeks.

*Patriotic themes adorn envelopes in a Federal's
writing kit (left). Vital to a soldier's morale, the U.S. Mail
was more reliable than that of the Confederacy.*

Wielding swords, bottles, and fists, Federal officers of Joe Hooker's staff stage a mock brawl while the man at right poses with a shovel to bury the "dead." To remain still for the long exposure, the swordsman at center holds onto the man at his left while he rests his weapon on the sword guard of his adversary.

The long, thin fife (top) was played along with clarinets, guitars, fiddles, and banjos to provide accompaniment to songfests and dances that broke the boredom of camp life. Music was immensely popular in the ranks and was so important to Confederate cavalry chief Jeb Stuart that he had a celebrated banjo player attached to his staff.

A musical ensemble displays their instruments — tambourine, banjo, guitar, violin, triangle, and bones.

As his messmates look on, a Federal soldier takes time out from chopping firewood beside a mud-chinked winter hut near Falls Church, Virginia, in February 1863. Two men peer from the window to the right of a former slave turned servant while the cook, or "dogrobber," as he was often called, wields pans and a large knife.

Father Thomas H. Mooney says mass for the Irish 69th New York near Arlington, Virginia, before the Battle of Bull Run in 1861. Religious literature was distributed among Yankee and Confederate troops, and on both sides the Bible was the most widely read of all books.

*Behind a Federal company standing at attention inside Fort Pulaski,
off-duty soldiers play baseball with handmade balls and bats like those
at left. The game became immensely popular during the war.*

Of Duty and Drill

Although each battle may have seemed to last an eternity to the soldier engaged in it, very little of his time was actually spent in fighting. Much more time went into preparing for combat. Most men had to be taught to be soldiers through boring repetition of forming and closing ranks, marching and countermarching — by the right flank, by the left flank — bayonet and skirmish drills, and loading and firing muskets and artillery pieces. There were roll calls, inspections, and long stints on sentry duty in all kinds of weather *(left)*. When not training, the men performed a wide variety of duties to maintain the machinery of war. Often they brought the skills needed for these tasks to camp from their civilian lives. There were engineers and carpenters to build and shore up bridges. There were farriers to shoe mules and horses, wheelwrights and blacksmiths to repair caissons, wagons, and ironclad vessels. There were telegraphers and signalmen for communications systems, and pick and shovel men to construct roads and keep them open. As they carried out these various duties, they sometimes stopped to freeze the action for the photographer's lens.

★

With their camp neatly spread out behind them, a Federal company drills high atop a hill behind Harpers Ferry, West Virginia. Following the war, the buildings would serve as the campus of Storer College, a school for freedmen.

Casually dressed and full of bravado, Confederate recruits drill at their large artillery piece in Pensacola, Florida. The swords of the two men at left moved during this exposure by J. D. Edwards.

In this photo by A. J. Russell, a Union work party repairs damage to the bridge across Bull Run near Manassas. During the war, the span, a vital rail link for supplies in north central Virginia, was destroyed six times by military action and once by flood.

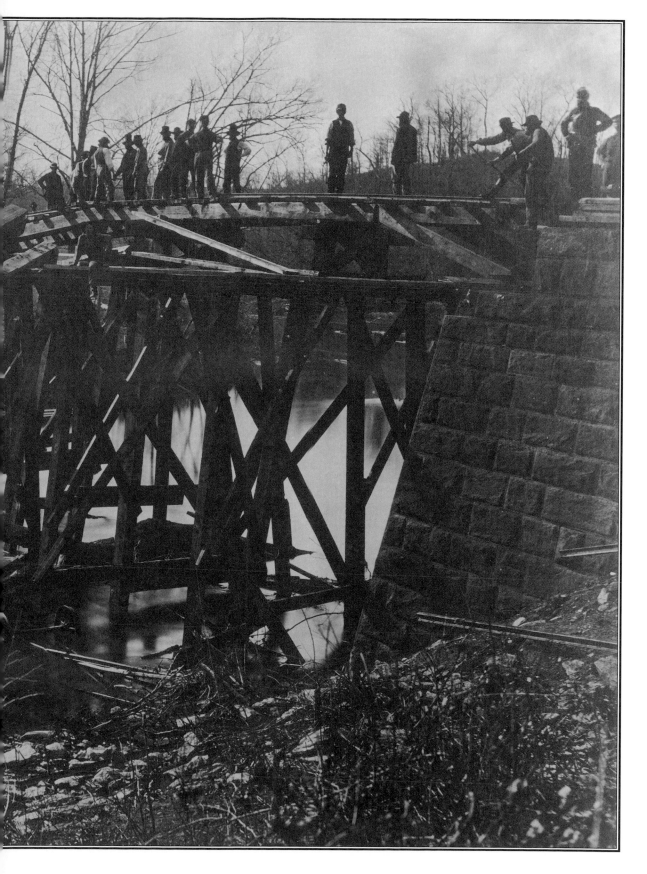

A company of the 40th Massachusetts practices the "Guard against Cavalry" stance during a bayonet drill near Washington, D.C. The "Guard against Infantry" position was similar, but the tip of the bayonet was held at belly, rather than at chin, level.

On the Potomac River waterfront at Alexandria, Virginia, Federal soldiers float a fieldpiece, its carriage, and a limber on an experimental barge made of wooden frames covered with rubberized cloth.

Wielding picks and spades, men of the 50th New York Engineers cut a road along the steep south bank of the North Anna River during Grant's drive toward Richmond in 1864.

In preparation for shoeing a cantankerous mule, farriers have winched the beast off the ground with a sling mechanism and immobilized its off hind leg, making it virtually impossible for the animal to resist.

Perched precariously atop freshly cut saplings, members of a telegraph construction crew prepare to string wire high enough to protect it from the bustling traffic below.

Federal sailors of the engineering gang aboard the Lehigh forge a replacement part on the deck of the iron-clad. Their portable forge and anvil, stand-ard equipment on monitors, were also used to repair dam-aged sheet armor.

A Federal brigade engages in a skirmish drill. In the foreground a skirmish line and its reserve lie prone to avoid hostile fire. The rest of the brigade is drawn up in battle lines. Artillery pieces appear at left in the background.

The Harvest of War

Although the limits of their craft kept them from stopping the action of actual combat and capturing it on plates, just as photographers had documented the prelude to battle, so, too, they documented its aftermath. This was different in many ways from their other work because the subjects could be moved and their accouterments rearranged to achieve a more powerful, artistic composition, and there was little chance that those "posing" would move to blur the image. At Antietam, Alexander Gardner took the first photos of American dead on a field of battle. More and more such images would be taken by many photographers as the war progressed and, like the one of a mass grave, trench reburial at left, even after the conflict had ended. When Gardner's images were first displayed at Mathew Brady's New York gallery in October 1862, the impact on the noncombatant public was stated clearly by one viewer: "We recognized the battlefield as a reality, but a remote one, like a funeral next door. Mr. Brady has brought home the terrible earnestness of war. If he has not brought bodies and laid them in our dooryard, he has done something very like it."

*In this image taken by
Alexander Gardner
near the Mumma farm
on September 19, 1862,
two days after the bloody
Battle of Antietam,
Confederate dead, gath-
ered for burial, appear
in a long sweeping arc
across a gentle slope.*

*Almost appearing as if taking a nap, a dead rebel soldier
lies in a shallow depression in another image taken by Gardner
on the battlefield near Sharpsburg, Maryland.*

A visitor to the Antietam battlefield described a scene matching the Gardner image below: "One beautiful milk-white animal had died in so graceful a position. . . . Its legs were doubled under and its arched neck gracefully turned to one side, as if looking back to the ball-hole in its side. . . . it was hard to believe the horse was dead."

Confederate dead sprawl in the Sunken Road on Marye's Heights where they fell during a spirited but doomed attempt to fend off a Yankee attack on May 3, 1863. A. J. Russell, who probably rearranged the bodies and their equipment for what he felt was a stronger effect, took this image the day after the attack.

A young Confederate soldier lies dead in a sharpshooter's nest in the Devil's Den at Gettysburg. The blanket beneath the man suggests that the photographer — probably Timothy O'Sullivan — moved the body to this spot before making the exposure.

★ ★ ★ In the course of this second of three intended five-year stints, the third of which will bring me to defeat and victory at Appomattox, my debt has grown heavier on both sides of the line where the original material leaves off, but most particularly on the near side of the line. Although the *Official Records,* supplemented by various other utterances by the participants, remain the primary source on which this narrative is based, the hundredth anniversary has enriched the store of comment on that contemporary evidence with biographies, studies of the conflict as a whole, examinations of individual campaigns, and general broodings on the minutiae — all of them, or anyhow nearly all of them, useful to the now dwindling number of writers and readers who, surviving exposure to the glut, continue to make that war their main historical concern. So that, while I agree in essence with Edmund Wilson's observation that "a day of mourning would be more appropriate," the celebration of the Centennial has at least been of considerable use to those engaged, as I am, in the process Robert Penn Warren has referred to as "picking the scab of our fate."

Not that my previous obligations have not continued. They have indeed, and they have been enlarged in the process. Kenneth P. Williams, Douglas Southall Freeman, J. G. Randall, Lloyd Lewis, Stanley F. Horn, Carl Sandburg, Bell I. Wiley, Bruce Catton, T. Harry Williams, Allan Nevins, Robert S. Henry, Jay Monaghan, E. Merton Coulter, Clifford Dowdey, Burton J. Hendrick, Margaret Leech are but a handful among the many to whom I am indebted as guides through the labyrinth. Without them I not only would have missed a great many wonders along the way, I would surely have been lost amid the intricate turnings and the uproar. Moreover, the debt continued to mount as the exploration proceeded: to Hudson Strode, for instance, for the extension of his *Jefferson Davis* at a time when the need was sore, and to Mark Mayo Boatner for his labor-saving *Civil War Dictionary.* Specific accounts of individual campaigns, lately published to expand or replace the more or less classical versions by Bigelow and others, have been of particular help through this relentless stretch of fighting. Edward J. Stackpole's *Chancellorsville,* for example, was used in conjunction with two recent biographies of the hero of that battle, Frank E. Vandiver's *Mighty Stonewall* and Lenoir Chambers' *Stonewall Jackson.* Similarly, for the Vicksburg campaign, there were Earl Schenck Miers' *The Web of Victory* and Peter F. Walker's *Vicksburg, a People at War,* plus biographies of the two commanders, *Pemberton, Defender of Vicksburg* and *Grant Moves South,* by John C. Pemberton and Bruce Catton. For Gettysburg, there were Clifford Dowdey's *Death of a Nation,* Glenn Tucker's *High Tide at Gettysburg,* and George R. Stewart's *Pickett's Charge.* For the battles around Chattanooga, there were Glenn Tucker's *Chickamauga* and Fairfax Downey's *Storming of the Gateway.* James M. Merrill's *The Rebel Shore,* Fletcher Pratt's *Civil War on Western Waters,* and Clarence E. Macartney's *Mr. Lincoln's Admirals* contributed to the naval actions, as Benjamin P. Thomas' and Harold M. Hyman's *Stanton* did to events in Washington. These too are only a few of the most recent among the many, old and new, on which I have drawn. Other obligations, of a more personal nature, were carried over from the outset: to the John Simon Guggenheim Memorial Foundation, which extended my fellowship beyond the norm: to the National Park Service, whose guides helped me (as they will you) to get to know so many confusing fields: to the William Alexander Percy Memorial Library, in my home town Greenville, Mississippi, which continued its loan of the *Official Records* and other reference works: to Robert D. Loomis of Random House, who managed to keep both his temper and his enthusiasm beyond unmet deadlines: to Memphis friends, who gave me food and whiskey without demanding payment in the form of talk about the war. To all these I am grateful: and to my wife Gwyn Rainer Foote, who bore with me.

Other, less specific obligations were as heavy. The photographs of Mathew Brady, affording as they do a gritty sense of participation — of being in the presence of the uniformed and frock-coated men who fought the battles and did the thinking, such as it was — gave me as much to go on, for example, as anything mentioned above. Further afield, but no less applicable, Richmond Lattimore's translation of the *Iliad* put a Greekless author in close touch with

★

his model. Indeed, to be complete, the list of my debts would have to be practically endless. Proust I believe has taught me more about the organization of material than even Gibbon has done, and Gibbon taught me much; Mark Twain and William Faulkner would also have to be included, for they left their sign on all they touched, and in the course of this exploration of the American scene I often found that they had been there before me. In a quite different sense, I am obligated also to the governors of my native state and the adjoining states of Arkansas and Alabama for helping to lessen my sectional bias by reproducing, in their actions during several of the years that went into the writing of this volume, much that was least admirable in the position my forebears occupied when they stood up to Lincoln. I suppose, or in any case fervently hope, it is true that history never repeats itself, but I know from watching these three gentlemen that it can be terrifying in its approximations, even when the reproduction — deriving, as it does, its scale from the performers — is in miniature.

As for method, it may explain much for me to state that my favorite historian is Tacitus, who dealt mainly with high-placed scoundrels, but that the finest compliment I ever heard paid a historian was tendered by Thomas Hobbes in the foreword to his translation of *The Peloponnesian War,* in which he referred to Thucydides as "one who, though he never digress to read a Lecture, Moral or Political, upon his own Text, nor enter into men's hearts, further than the Actions themselves evidently guide him . . . yet filleth his Narrations with that choice of matter, and ordereth them with that Judgement, and with such perspicuity and efficacy expresseth himself that (as Plutarch saith) he maketh his Auditor a Spectator. For he setteth his Reader in the Assemblies of the People, and in their Senates, at their debating; in the Streets, at their Seditions; and in the Field, at their Battels." There indeed is something worth aiming at, however far short of attainment we fall.

S.F.

Picture Credits

Dust jacket: Front, National Archives, Neg. No. B-189; **rear,** Library of Congress, Neg. No. B8184-10006; **flap,** Larry Shirkey. **8-10:** Massachusetts Commandery Military Order of the Loyal Legion and the U.S. Army Military History Institute (MASS-MOLLUS/USAMHI). **12-15:** Frank and Marie-Thérèse Wood Print Collections, Alexandria, Va. **17:** Library of Congress, Neg. No. B817 7345. **20:** Frank and Marie-Thérèse Wood Print Collections, Alexandria, Va. **26:** Courtesy William Gladstone Collection. **35:** Painting by William Edward West, Washington/Custis/Lee Collection, Washington and Lee University, Lexington, Va., photographed by Thomas C. Bradshaw II. **39:** National Portrait Gallery, Smithsonian Institution/Art Resource. **42-44:** From *The Photographic History of the Civil War,* Vol. 6, Review of Reviews Co., New York, 1911. **48:** Naval Historical Center, Department of the Navy, courtesy General Dynamics Corp., Electric Boat Division. **50, 51:** Museum of the Confederacy, Richmond, photographed by Larry Sherer. **53:** MASS-MOLLUS/USAMHI, copied by A. Pierce Bounds. **54, 55:** From *The Photographic History of the Civil War,* Vol. 6, Review of Reviews Co., New York, 1911. **59:** Western Reserve Historical Society, Cleveland. **64:** Courtesy Chris Nelson. **67:** Library of Congress, Waud Collection. **72:** National Archives, Neg. No. 111-B-6209—courtesy Don Troiani, photographed by Al Freni. **74:** National Archives, RG94, Union Battle Reports, courtesy James O. Hall. **76-83:** Frank and Marie-Thérèse Wood Print Collections, Alexandria, Va. **87:** From *The Photographic History of the Civil War,* Vol. 10, Review of Reviews Co., New York, 1911. **90:** Michael J. Winey Collection at USAMHI. **94, 95:** Frank and Marie-Thérèse Wood Print Collections, Alexandria, Va. **98:** From *The Photographic History of the Civil War,* Vol. 10, Review of Reviews Co., New York, 1911. **103:** Frank and Marie-Thérèse Wood Print Collections, Alexandria, Va. **106:** Courtesy Lloyd Ostendorf Collection. **108-110:** National Archives, Neg. No. 90-CM-289. **113:** Courtesy Lloyd Ostendorf Collection. **116:** National Archives, Neg. No. 111-B-2886. **121:** Frank and Marie-Thérèse Wood Print Collections, Alexandria, Va. **125:** Library of Congress, Neg. No. 15508-BH832-304. **129:** Alabama Department of Archives and History, Montgomery. **133:** Courtesy Chris Nelson. **136:** Courtesy the Trustees of the Boston Public Library. **138:** Sophia Smith Collection, Women's History Archive, Smith College (SATSI). **140-142:** Orlando Poe Collection, Special Collections, U.S. Military Academy Library, copied by Henry Groskinsky. **145:** Courtesy William C. Davis. **150:** Library of Congress Neg. No. 3217 B8184 651. **152:** Western Reserve Historical Society, Cleveland—courtesy William J. Prince. **153:** Library of Congress, Neg. No. BH8277-550. **154:** Courtesy William Gladstone Collection. **156:** From *Still More Confederate Faces,* by Domenick Serrano, Metropolitan Co., Bayside, N.Y. 1992—courtesy Jim Stamatelos; courtesy Larry B. Williford. **157:** Russel J. Wunker Collection/USAMHI, copied by Robert Walch; courtesy William J. Prince—courtesy Larry B. Williford. **158:** Courtesy William J. Prince—Division of Archives and Manuscripts, Pennsylvania Historical and Museum Commission/USAMHI, copied by Robert Walch. **159:** Courtesy William J. Prince—courtesy Richard K. Tibbals. **160:** Courtesy Mildred Pickle Mayhall, copied by Bill Malone; courtesy T. Sherman Harding—courtesy Larry B. Williford. **161:** Courtesy Larry B. Williford-USAMHI, copied by Robert Walch. **162:** Western Reserve Historical Society, Cleveland. **164, 165:** Library of Congress, Neg. No. 26543 B8171 625; courtesy Chris Nelson. **166, 167:** The Lightfoot Collection, Greenport, N.Y. **168, 169:** Library of Congress, Neg. No. B8184-7145; Nelsonian Institute, photographed by Larry Sherer. **170, 171:** Library of Congress. **172, 173:** Courtesy Don Troiani, photographed by Henry Groskinsky; MASS-MOLLUS/USAMHI, copied by A. Pierce Bounds. **174, 175:** Library of Congress, Neg. No. BN8255-91. **176, 177:** From *Dear Friends, The Civil War Letters and Diary of Charles Edwin Cort,* comp. and ed. with commentaries by Helyn W. Tomlinson, 1962, copied by Philip Brandt George—Museum of the Confederacy, Richmond, photographed by Larry Sherer (2); Museum of the Confederacy, Richmond, photographed by Katherine Wetzel. **178, 179:** National Archives, Neg. No. 111-B-252. **180, 181:** Library of Congress, Neg. No. B8184 4132—Eleanor S. Brockenbrough Library/Museum of the Confederacy, Richmond. **182:** Stamatelos Brothers Collection, photographed by Andrew K. Howard; Western Reserve Historical Society, Cleveland. **184:**

National Archives, Neg. No. 111-B-7029. **186, 187:** National Park Service, Harpers Ferry, W.Va. **188, 189:** From *The Photographic History of the Civil War,* Vol. 8, Review of Reviews Co., New York, 1911. **190, 191:** The Huntington Library, Clough Collection, San Marino, Calif. **192, 193:** Western Reserve Historical Society, Cleveland. **194, 195:** National Archives, Neg. No. 77-F-194-6-80. **196, 197:** Library of Congress, Neg. No. B8184 749. **198, 199:** Albert Shaw Collection, Review of Reviews, *Photographic*

History of the Civil War, copied by Larry Sherer. **200, 201:** Library of Congress, Neg. No. B8184 4196. **202, 203:** National Archives, Neg. No. 111-B-611. **204, 205:** MASS-MOLLUS/USAMHI, copied by Robert Walch. **206:** National Archives, Neg. No. 165-A-446. **208:** Library of Congress, Neg. No. 21370 B811 557. **210, 211:** Library of Congress, Neg. No. B 811-554—Library of Congress, Neg. No. 21367 B8184-558. **212, 213:** National Archives. **214, 215:** National Archives, Neg. No. 165-SB-41.

Index

SHELBY FOOTE, THE CIVIL WAR,
A NARRATIVE
VOLUME 9 MINE RUN TO MERIDIAN

Library of Congress Cataloging-in-Publication Data
Foote, Shelby.
   [Civil War, a narrative]
   Shelby Foote, the Civil War, a narrative / by Shelby
Foote and the editors of Time-Life Books. — 40th
Anniversary ed.
         p. cm.
   Originally published: The Civil War, a narrative.
New York : Random House, 1958-1974, in 3 v.
   Includes bibliographical references and indexes.
   Contents: v. 9. Mine Run to Meridian
   ISBN 0-7835-0108-0
   1. United States—History—Civil War, 1861-1865.
I. Time-Life Books. II. Title.
E468.F7 1999   99-13486
973.7—dc21   CIP

10 9 8 7 6 5 4 3 2 1

OTHER TIME-LIFE HISTORY PUBLICATIONS

For information on and a full description of any of
the Time-Life Books series listed above, please call
1-800-621-7026 or write:
Reader Information
Time-Life Customer Service
P.O. Box C-32068
Richmond, Virginia 23261-2068

Time-Life Books is a
division of Time Life Inc.

TIME LIFE INC.
PRESIDENT and CEO: Jim Nelson

TIME-LIFE BOOKS
PUBLISHER/MANAGING EDITOR: Neil Kagan
SENIOR VICE PRESIDENT, MARKETING:
Joseph A. Kuna
VICE PRESIDENT, NEW PRODUCT
DEVELOPMENT: Amy Golden

PROJECT EDITOR: Philip Brandt George
Art Director: Ellen L. Pattisall
Copyeditor: Kimberly A. Grandcolas
Editorial Assistant: Patricia D. Whiteford
Photo Coordinator: Susan L. Finken

Special Contributors: Constance B. Contreras
(research); John Drummond, Jennifer A. Gearhart,
Belen Price (design and production); Roy Nanovic
(index)

Correspondent: Christina Lieberman (New York)

Separations by the Time-Life Imaging Department

NEW PRODUCT DEVELOPMENT: Director,
Elizabeth D. Ward; Project Manager, Karen Inge-
bretsen; Director of Marketing, Mary Ann Donaghy;
Marketing Manager, Paul Fontaine; Associate Marketing Manager, Erin Gaskins

MARKETING: Director, Peter Tardif; Marketing
Manager, Nancy Gallo; Associate Marketing
Manager, Kristen N. O'Shea

Executive Vice President, Operations: Ralph Cuomo
Senior Vice President and CFO: Claudia Goldberg
Senior Vice President, Law & Business Affairs:
Randolph H. Elkins

Vice President, Financial Planning & Analysis:
Christopher Hearing
Vice President, Book Production: Patricia Pascale
Vice President, Imaging: Marjann Caldwell
Director, Publishing Technology: Betsi McGrath
Director, Editorial Administration: Barbara Levitt
Director, Photography and Research:
John Conrad Weiser
Director, Quality Assurance: James King
Manager, Technical Services: Anne Topp
Senior Production Manager: Ken Sabol
Manager, Copyedit/Page Makeup: Debby Tait
Chief Librarian: Louise D. Forstall